# CUTTING
# HUMOUR

D0543553

**This book contains yet another selection of the misprints and absurdities culled from the press by PRIVATE EYE.**

**The majority were sent in by readers to whom our thanks are due.**

# PRIVATE EYE'S

# CUTTING HUMOUR

Illustrated by
ROBERT THOMPSON

PRIVATE EYE · CORGI

Published in Great Britain by
Private Eye Productions Ltd
6 Carlisle Street, London W1V 5RG
in association with Corgi Books

©1993 Pressdram Ltd
ISBN 0 552 14179 8

Designed by Bridget Tisdall
Printed in England by
Clays Ltd, St Ives plc

Corgi Books are published by Transworld Publishers Ltd
61-63 Uxbridge Road, Ealing, London W5 5SA
in Australia by Transworld Publishers (Australia) Pty, Ltd
15-25 Helles Avenue, Moorebank, NSW 2170
and in New Zealand by Transworld Publishers (N.Z.) Ltd
3 William Pickering Drive, Albany, Auckland

10 9 8 7 6 5 4 3 2 1

PC Nick Shaw, with his wife Louise, after they had seen their home wrecked by a gas explosion.

*The Times*

## Avril Poat

We would like to clarify an article which appeared in the Richmond and Twickenham Times three weeks ago.

We wish to make it clear that Avril Poat, of Whitton Dene, pleaded guilty to driving with excess alcohol at Richmond Magistrates Court and not to being a drunken woman motorist.

*Daily Telegraph*

## Rare eggs hoard

Police seized 1,500 rare birds' eggs from a house in Mosborough, Sheffield. A man has been questioned about a suspected poaching operation.

*Daily Telegraph*

Wednesday, Thursday and Friday Evenings
— **Uwe Fock entertains on the Organ in the Dining Room**

*Advertisement in Niugini Nius (Papua New Guinea)*

During yesterday's proceedings Miss Tan — real name Miss Bonkers — tried on a sexy black corset in the witness-box at Southwark Crown Court to prove it didn't fit her 5ft 4in. figure.

*The Star*

THE army was called in after a major security alert at Chesterfield's divisional police hindquarters.

*Chesterfield Gazette*

**LETCHWORTH SPIRITUALIST CHURCH GERNON WALK**
**An evening of Clairvoyance**
**with Mr H. Deadmen**
Saturday, July 27, at 7 pm
**Admission 75p**
c3n30

*Stevenage Express*

**—Personal—**

EX-LONDON Publican seeks lady with pub. Send photo of pub. Tel:

*Morning Advertiser*

Since hospitalisation may no longer be considered a viable option for the majority of cases, forms of community care and assessment will have to found, thus shifting the anus from psychiatric to community orientated assessment.

*Community Care*

# Raider fled after bite by 'Dracula'

*Yorkshire Post*

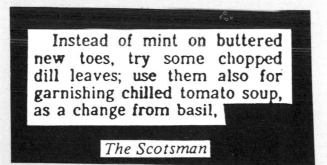

Instead of mint on buttered new toes, try some chopped dill leaves; use them also for garnishing chilled tomato soup, as a change from basil,

*The Scotsman*

Supt John McKay said: "We will be out in force that night, intending to maintain law and order. Our officers will balance tolerance and firmness – but any outbreaks of public order will be dealt with swiftly.

*Grantham Journal*

**DEREK JAMESON:**
**Morning show axed**

Popular BBC radio broadcaster Derek Jameson, 81, has been told that, after five years, his peak-time BBC Radio 2 morning show is to be dropped.

*Hello!*

**3** The Red Crap Apple Tree. Bright red colours. Gives a massive number of flowers during April/ May and plenty of Crab Apples during late summer.

◇ ◆ 4 5 ✄
YG 619- One tree          £12.50

*Advertisement*

Mr. Dundas in his own country has been something like *the pelican in the wilderness*; nothing but fuck, fuck, fuck; fuck, fuck, fuck; and for *the very blood of him*, he has not been able to satisfy all his relations———

*The Observer, December 4, 1791*

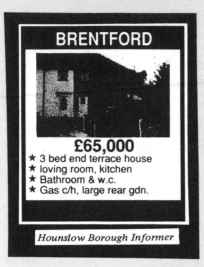
## CAVENDISH EDUCATIONAL CONSULTANTS

The above named student has quated our office adress for correspondence. We would be grateful if you could ammend your records and send all future information, such as accomodation, joining instruction atc.) to the new adress below.

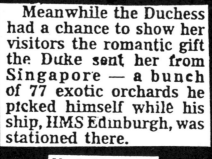

Meanwhile the Duchess had a chance to show her visitors the romantic gift the Duke sent her from Singapore — a bunch of 77 exotic orchards he picked himself while his ship, HMS Edinburgh, was stationed there.

*Yorkshire Post*

£1,950. 'V' Fiat X19 Sports car, requiring attention £750. 'T' Ford Escort 1.1L, £475. Lots of cheaper cars! All usual dealer facilities! Hire cars £17.50 daily, all in ! University Autos, Occupation Road, Cambridge, phone 313400 or 67774! Millie (that's Jonny's mum) an ex Kite resident also lost her part time cleaning job at WW offals' restaurant when City Council demolished the whole area to make way for the Grafton Centre! Now that she has heard about the proposed development on New Street / East Roadarea she is livid! She says this time it's Jonny's job on the line! She is asking all those who live or work in this area to attend the public meeting on Tuesday, February 6th, at 7.00pm, at Howard Mallets Club and oppose to this senseless devastation! She say's she don't want any more Grafton Centre or shops that sell £1.25 Cornish pasties! or £10 a day car parks! She wants to work for the community not for London developers!.

*Cambridge Evening News*

*Can label, Ghana*

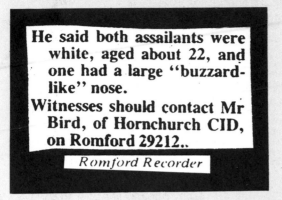

He said both assailants were white, aged about 22, and one had a large "buzzard-like" nose.

Witnesses should contact Mr Bird, of Hornchurch CID, on Romford 29212..

*Romford Recorder*

**7.30  HE MAKES ME FEEL LIKE DANCING**
Academy-award winning documentary in which Jacques d'Amboise, principal dancer of the New York City Ballet, leads a thousand children in his annual gaga performance.

*Bradford Telegraph and Argus*

Howard Brentone. He caused uproar with his steamy London play Romans in Brighton, which featured a homosexual rape.

*The Mirror*

**BRAND NEW** three pink bridesmaids, dresses plus accessories £35 each. 764 6893

*Wimbledon Guardian*

The regulations, introduced by the former health minister, Mr Kenneth Clarke, mean doctors can apply to courts for orders forcing Aids patients to undergo a medical examination and/or be kept in hospital against their will if they are a pubic health risk.

*Grauniad*

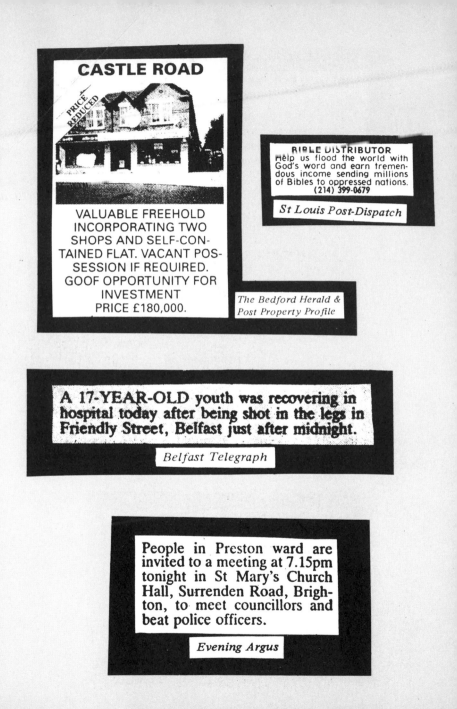

**CASTLE ROAD**

*PRICE REDUCED*

VALUABLE FREEHOLD
INCORPORATING TWO
SHOPS AND SELF-CON-
TAINED FLAT. VACANT POS-
SESSION IF REQUIRED.
GOOF OPPORTUNITY FOR
INVESTMENT
PRICE £180,000.

*The Bedford Herald &
Post Property Profile*

A 17-YEAR-OLD youth was recovering in
hospital today after being shot in the legs in
Friendly Street, Belfast just after midnight.

*Belfast Telegraph*

People in Preston ward are
invited to a meeting at 7.15pm
tonight in St Mary's Church
Hall, Surrenden Road, Brighton, to meet councillors and
beat police officers.

*Evening Argus*

Regulations setting minimum quality standards should be consistent with EC standards although dispensations have been issued by the Secretary of State for the Environment allowing all ten water authorities to continue supplying water which contravenes EC standards. Undertakers will be required to keep records of the quality of water supplied and to conduct regular sampling regimes, the result of which must be publicly available.

*European Newsletter*
*Nabarro Nathanson*

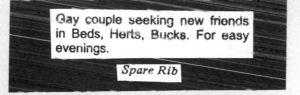

Gay couple seeking new friends in Beds, Herts, Bucks. For easy evenings.

*Spare Rib*

**Yorkshire crowds have been accused of racist behaviour towards black players in recent years. But the club's new chief executive, Chris Hassell, stressed that he had imported the idea from Lancashire, where he was formerly secretary.**

*Daily Telegraph*

# CHANCE TO MEET MR UNIVERSE

*Cumbrian Gazette*

AFTER trying to strangle his wife in their Ilchester home Brian John Masters called the police and asked for help.

*Yeovil & District Western Gazette*

Town boss John Maggs had big defender Tommy Warrilow back in the heart of defence following a groin injury, but was missing striker Frank Ovard out with a badly bruised rectum.

*Crawley News*

### CROGLIN

At the December meeting, Mrs. Todd, a deitician, spoke on "You are what you eat". She was thanked by Mrs F. Dixon.

The competition for mince pies was won by Mrs. M. Dixon.

*Cumberland & Westmoreland Herald*

The workshop will be taken by celebrated director John Sichel who has mounted stage, screen and TV productions round the world and has bad actors of the calibre of Laurence Olivier, Alan Bates and Alec Guinness in his casts.

*Focus*

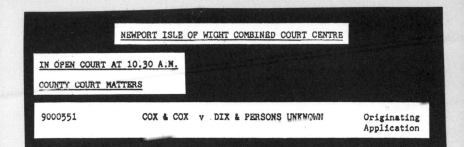

NEWPORT ISLE OF WIGHT COMBINED COURT CENTRE

IN OPEN COURT AT 10.30 A.M.

COUNTY COURT MATTERS

9000551          COX & COX   v . DIX & PERSONS UNKNOWN          Originating Application

**Captain fights suit**

Captain Mark Phillips has announced he will contest a paternity suit against him in New Zealand. **Page 2; Equestrian events, page 27**

*Grauniad*

YOU report (March 24) that I was held for 24 hours by Munich police after a rally there last April. In fact I was held for only a couple of hours, largely taken up by police officials asking me to autograph books.

*Letter from David Irving*
*Sunday Telegraph*

Kelly confirmed that recommendations that obscene chanting, the throwing of missiles, trespass onto pitches, and the activities of touts outside grounds on match days, received the full endorsement of the football authorities.

*The Times*

## Call for party to disown Proctor

THE Confederation of Indian Organisations in the United Kingdom has formally asked for the Conservative whip to be withdrawn from Mr Harvey Proctor, MP for Billericay.

*The Guardian*

## Changing of the Guard

The Household Cavalry Regiment mounts The Queen's Life Guard at **Horse Guards**, 11am.

*The Times*

▲ In flight service includes meals

*El Al Superstars Holidays brochure*

Gays and lesbians are now being openly encouraged by Labour authorities like Lambeth, Stephen Green of Streatham Conservatives told a party rally.

And in Lambeth social workers and staff are now positively recruited on the strength of their interest in buggery.

"This loophole must be sewn up," he added.

*South London News*

For dessert, Christmas pudding and brandy butter or mice pie and cream, followed by a selection of English and French cheeses, biscuits and celery. All very reasonable for £9.25 a head.

**Waltham Forest Guardian**

The DoT intended scrapping the regulations which required separate sleeping rooms to be provided, said Kinahan, and allowing owners to allocated two ratings or pretty officers to share a cabin on vessels over 25,000 gross tons built since July 1979.

*N.U.S. Magazine*

# Thatcher's role

Giving her views on "The Englishwoman's Wardrobe," to be shown on BBC2 in November, Mrs Thatcher says: "It's not my job to be a fashion leader, but it is my job to be out of fashion or obviously wrongly dressed."

*Daily Telegraph*

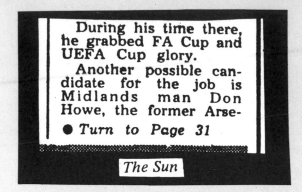

During his time there, he grabbed FA Cup and UEFA Cup glory.

Another possible candidate for the job is Midlands man Don Howe, the former Arse-

● *Turn to Page 31*

*The Sun*

Lord Longford, the social campaigner has defended Hindley's right to be considered for parole on the grounds that he has been converted to Roman Catholicism, and now regrets the killings.

*Daily Telegraph*

**BONE — MARROW** — The engagement is announced between Joanne Louise, only daughter of Mr and Mrs D. Marrow, 295 Bury Road and Kevin James Bone, only son of Mr and Mrs J. Bone, 41

*Bury Times*

**ANTIQUE** piano with candelabra and spiral staircase etc.

*Edinbugh Advertiser*

**PASTA SALAD** mixed with either chunks of fish or baby, barely cooked broad beans, then dressed with oil and vinegar, is very good, too.

*The Irish Times*

Mr Longden opened the case by asking the jury to put out of their nids anything they may previously have heard or read about Cynthia Payne.

*Daily Telegraph*

Group Support Services     B. M. Cocup     – Group Personnel

*Midland Bank PLC Annual Report*

**7.0     Top of the Pops**, Blur, Cher, Seal and Roxette to name just the monosyllables appearing.

*Grauniad*

119 BAD BARGAIN LANE, YORK     £31,950 to include all carpets

*Wells Cundall Property Guide*

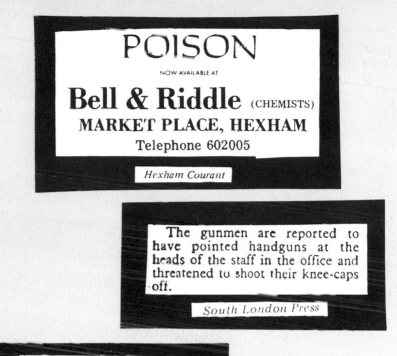

# POISON

NOW AVAILABLE AT

# Bell & Riddle (CHEMISTS)
## MARKET PLACE, HEXHAM
Telephone 602005

*Hexham Courant*

The gunmen are reported to have pointed handguns at the heads of the staff in the office and threatened to shoot their knee-caps off.

*South London Press*

HAMPTON residents woke up on Tuesday to flooding and traffic chaos when a waiter burst in the early hours of the morning.

*The Richmond and Twickenham Times.*

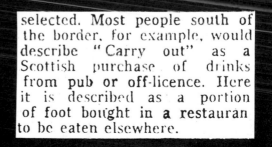

selected. Most people south of the border, for example, would describe "Carry out" as a Scottish purchase of drinks from pub or off-licence. Here it is described as a portion of foot bought in a restauran to be eaten elsewhere.

*Daily Telegraph*

**23 August - 11 September**
9:00am Daily except Saturdays. Finals held on Friday
of each week.

# GREAT YARMOUTH OPEN
# BOWELS FESTIVAL
Great Yarmouth Bowling Greens, Marine Parade,

*What's on, When
and Where
East Anglia*

A PAINTING bought for £5
which hung on a living room
wall for years was sold at
auction by Phillips in London
yesterday for £847,000. The 400-
year-old picture of St Lucy offering the Madonna and child a
couple of eyes, by Annibale
Carracci, belonged to the wife
of a Dorset designer.

*Grauniad*

**BUCK up, bosses!** Your
women workers are demand-
ing better treatment.

The tough message came yesterday from a plain-speaking
woman who has scaled the
heights of success — with maybe
the odd tumble on the way.

Edwina Currie, one of only 41
female MPs, predicted that by 1995
four out of every five new jobs will be
filled by women.

*Daily Express*

# REWARD.
Did you remove a lady from
Pitstone on Saturday
October 3rd. If so please
contact.
**Aylesbury 668252 or
0836 515386.**

gr45

*Towcester & Banbury Advertiser*

*Crossword solution, Today 5.3.'92*

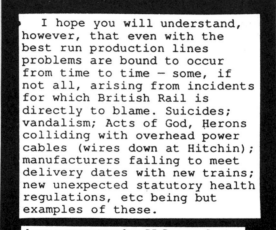

I hope you will understand, however, that even with the best run production lines problems are bound to occur from time to time — some, if not all, arising from incidents for which British Rail is directly to blame. Suicides; vandalism; Acts of God, Herons colliding with overhead power cables (wires down at Hitchin); manufacturers failing to meet delivery dates with new trains; new unexpected statutory health regulations, etc being but examples of these.

*Letter to a passenger from BR Customer Services*

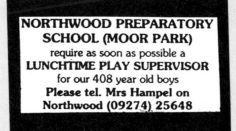

**NORTHWOOD PREPARATORY SCHOOL (MOOR PARK)**
require as soon as possible a
**LUNCHTIME PLAY SUPERVISOR**
for our 408 year old boys
**Please tel. Mrs Hampel on Northwood (09274) 25648**

**1.50pm** The host with the Midas touch, Henry Kelly, proves all that glisters really is gold

*Radio Times*

1.05 am **Movie:** Lets Love Each Other (1987) (Serbia/Croatia) (AO). 2.35 **Close.**

*Courier Messenger*

Jenkins, 29, admitted a charge of assault causing actual bodily harm and criminal damage to a telephone box.

*Wells Journal*

### MARTINI VERMOUTH

**Martini - What is it?**

Martini is a vermouth, one of the oldest types of drink in the world. It is a wine to which herbs, spices and other natural ingredients, including woodworm, have been added.

*Westbay 1992 Diary*

*Business card*

**A CHANGE of heart by education secretary Kenneth Baker lifted a threat to the future of Albury's village school of 20 pupils**

A daft circular from the government was urging the closure of primary schools with less than three staff,

*Herts & Essex Observer*

Even strippers' efforts to get around the nudity law by wearing see-through pasties failed. "We get them for simulating nudity," says the police chief, Rick Huck.

*Wall Street Journal*

# Coining it in

A mile of pennises collection in the Old George Mall, Salisbury, during August raised £250 for Guide Dogs for the Blind.

*Salisbury Journal*

"By common consent, these were males prostituting themselves for money — people at the bottom end of their trade — brought to this man by a rent boy agency. There is no question at all of corruption."

*The Times*

**DYNAMIC YOUNG SINGER REQUIRED**

**FOR MAJOR PART IN FILM**

Must be 25 or Under Male

**Auditions-2p.m. Friday 1st November**

**Electric Ballroom Camden High St. N.W.1**

*Advertisement, London Standard*

**The DEWAN-E-KHAS** Restaurant in Trowbridge is an exotic Indian oasis where you can find excellent authentic Indian dishes in a friendly hospital atmosphere. We look forward to welcoming you and your friends soon.

*Chippenham & Corsham Star*

**MI5 'used' Eye**

JOURNALISTS who have worked on Private eye believe that it was sued by the Security Services to spread smears against the Wilson government in the mid-1970s.

*Grauniad*

**Be There ! ! !**

*THE LIGHT HOUSE*

*COFFEE SHOP*

*by*

*THE POOL TERRACE*

*OVER LOOKING THE SEA*

*A LA CRATE MENU*

*Mount Lavinia Hotel, Sri Lanka*

PRESIDENT EVREN
REASSERTS TURKEY'S
STAND ON CYPRUS

*KIBRIS (Northern Cyprus Weekly)*

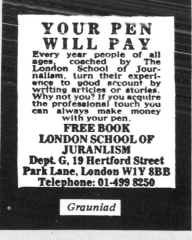

# YOUR PEN WILL PAY

**Every year people of all ages, coached by The London School of Journalism, turn their experience to good account by writing articles or stories. Why not you? If you acquire the professional touch you can always make money with your pen.**

**FREE BOOK
LONDON SCHOOL OF JURANLISM
Dept. G, 19 Hertford Street
Park Lane, London W1Y 8BB
Telephone: 01-499 8250**

*Grauniad*

"If they are saying it is wrong for homosexuals to teach in schools, are they saying it is wrong for homosexuals to seek the leadership of this country and prominent positions within this House?"

Mr Straw had insisted: "It is notorious that there are a number of members of the Conservative Party in Parliament,

*Edinburgh Evening News*

## CHARITY WORM SCOFF IS OFF!

A fundraiser scrapped his plan to eat a slimy seawater ragworm inch by inch for charity last night after a storm of protests.

The chew-in was one of a series of events at Lee, Hants, for Barnardo kids. An RSPCA officer said: "This is tasteless."

*The Sun*

**12.00—NIGHT COURT**
**12.30—PAGES FROM SKYTEXT**
Comedy series.

*Dublin Evening Herald*

£600,000 CUT — savings on running costs by selling off 12 old peoples to private buyers.

*Bradford Telegraph & Argus*

At night the flavour changes as Turkish women don't tend to come out at night. Their absence has probably got something to do with the awful organ music that seems so popular here. It takes little persuasion for another tone deaf Turk to leap up in a lokanta and wildly pump his organ, singing incomprehensible words in between gasps for air.

*Lancaster Travel*

A Sheffield barmaid who has spent 27 years collecting glasses and pulling pints took tea with the Duke of Devonshire and toured his home Chatsworth House. The visit was organised for Mrs Joan Senior, aged 59, by the landlord of the pub as a special retirement present.

*Yorkshire Evening Press*

*Clare Dyer adds:* Death by hanging was the penalty for murder in mainland Britain until 1965, when it was temporarily suspended. Suspension was made permanent in 1970.

*Grauniad*

# I'm not ready to quit yet, says BBC boss

BBC boss Sir Michael Checkland yesterday denied that he would be quitting at the end of the year.

*Daily Mail*

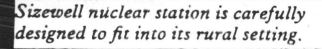

*Sizewell nuclear station is carefully designed to fit into its rural setting.*

**Reader's Digest**

# Assault

Alexander James Gallacher (32), 53 Comrie Street, Crieff, had sentence deferred until December 9 at Perth Sheriff Court today.

He admitted that on March 6 in his home he assaulted his wife Linda, pulled her hair, repeatedly punched and kicked her on the head arms and body to her injury.

Sentence was deferred for his good behaviour.

*Dundee Evening Telegraph*

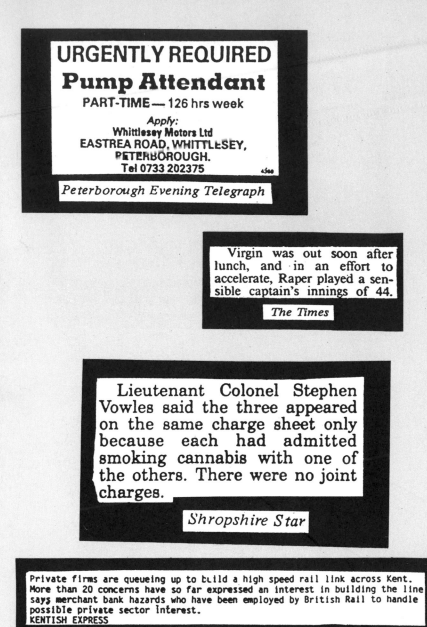

## URGENTLY REQUIRED
## Pump Attendant
**PART-TIME — 126 hrs week**

*Apply:*
**Whittlesey Motors Ltd
EASTREA ROAD, WHITTLESEY,
PETERBOROUGH.
Tel 0733 202375**

*Peterborough Evening Telegraph*

Virgin was out soon after lunch, and in an effort to accelerate, Raper played a sensible captain's innings of 44.

*The Times*

Lieutenant Colonel Stephen Vowles said the three appeared on the same charge sheet only because each had admitted smoking cannabis with one of the others. There were no joint charges.

*Shropshire Star*

Private firms are queueing up to build a high speed rail link across Kent. More than 20 concerns have so far expressed an interest in building the line says merchant bank hazards who have been employed by British Rail to handle possible private sector interest.
KENTISH EXPRESS

*Kent County Council weekly news digest*

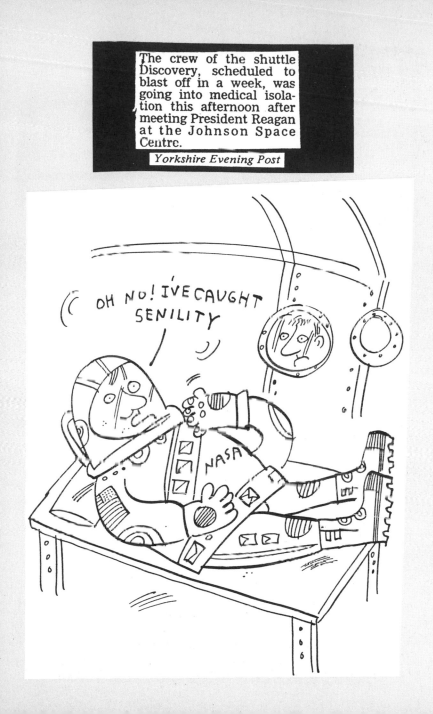

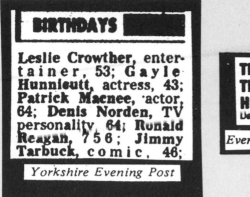

**FOR SALE BY PRIVATE TREATY
AS A GOING CONCERN**

# KIELDER FERRIES

*An established family run Ferry and Cruise
business on Kielder Water, Northumberland*

This highly profitable business is at the
moment being run by a husband and wife
team and enjoys the soul ferrying rights on
Kielder Water, now one of the
Northumberland's largest tourist
attractions.
Genuine reason for sale.

*Newcastle Journal*

---

Mrs Calder-Smith said in
her letter, published yesterday, that her daughter was
represented as "nothing more
than a feelingless sex kitchen".

*Sunday Times*

---

Police later arrested Bailey because they were suspicious of the
strangely stilted way he spoke to
them — as though he were a police
officer giving evidence in court.

*Gloucestershire Echo*

**BROMLEY** £61,000

- Attractive terrace house
- Three god size bedrooms
- Lounge, gas fire
- Fully fitted kitchen
- Bathroom, separate w.c.
- Detached double garage
- 60ft. rear garden

*Bromley & District Property News*

Mr. Moore, 50, was taken ill after a meeting with the Prime Minister. He left Downing Street doubled up in pain, and was rushed to Parkside Private Hospital, Wimbledon.

*The Star*

# Crash rider pronounced dead says 'Corfu medical treatment was terrible'

*Henley Standard*

**5.10-5.35pm Archer's Goon**

NEW The first in a six-part children's drama. The Goon comes to Howard's house demanding Archer's £2,000. But who is Archer?

*Radio Times*

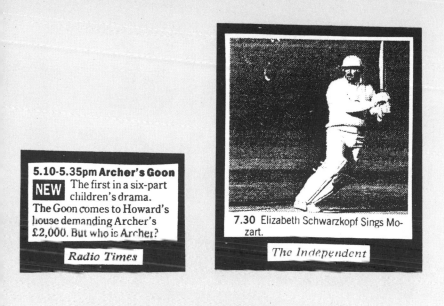

7.30 Elizabeth Schwarzkopf Sings Mozart.

*The Independent*

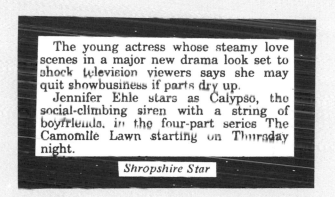

The young actress whose steamy love scenes in a major new drama look set to shock television viewers says she may quit showbusiness if parts dry up.

Jennifer Ehle stars as Calypso, the social-climbing siren with a string of boyfriends, in the four-part series The Camomile Lawn starting on Thursday night.

*Shropshire Star*

**Do a Rough Draft**

If you first write your application in draft, it will avoid mistakes and repitition and ensure that the final version is well organised, well presented and relevant.

*Tower Hamlets Education Authority*

# 28pc RISE IN COST OF NEW ROADS

THE COST of building new roads has fallen by a staggering 28 per cent this decade, according to Government figures published this week.

*Construction News*

# Mrs J Walker

IN our report of August 7, headlined "Toni's brush with untidy decorators", we referred to Mrs Jessie Walker, of Euston Avenue, Blackley, Manchester, as "blind and crippled". We have been asked to point out that Mrs Walker is, in fact, partially-sighted and severely disabled.

*Manchester Evening News*

# Spotted

Mr John Locke, prosecuting, said Dobbin was disqualified for 20 years in November 1981 for driving with excess alcohol, but in August this year magistrates reinstated his licence after an appeal.

He said on October 29 police spotted a car driving a pub.

Dobbin was arrested after he failed to supply a specimen of breath.

*Evening Mail*

*The Times*

Dr I.L.C. Sly
and Miss N.J.E. Fox
The engagement is announced between Ian, younger son of the late Capt L.T. Sly and of Mrs A.G. Sly, of Canterbury, Kent, and Nikola, only daughter of Mr and Mrs N.E. Fox, of Great Bealings, Suffolk.

*Press and Journal*

**Eggs 89/437/EEC**

Draft Egg Products Regulations.

Regulations are expected to be laid before Parliament by the end of the month.

*Environmental Health News*

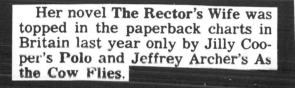

Her novel **The Rector's Wife** was topped in the paperback charts in Britain last year only by Jilly Cooper's **Polo** and Jeffrey Archer's **As the Cow Flies**.

*South African Sunday Times*

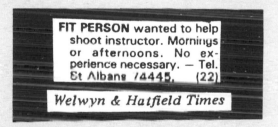

**FIT PERSON** wanted to help shoot instructor. Mornings or afternoons. No experience necessary. — Tel. St Albans 74445. (22)

*Welwyn & Hatfield Times*

DENIS HEALEY COMMUNITY CENTRE
Foundry Mill Street, Seacroft, Leeds 14

PART-TIME CLEANER

£2,4551 per hour

*Leeds City Council Dept. of Education*

Left: the listeria monocytogenes bacterium

Right: A colony of salmonella enteritidis bacteria

**BATTLE TO BEAT THE FOOD BUGS**
*Daily Telegraph*

# First leg over in BMA elections

*BMA News Review*

5.0 PM: news magazine. 5.55 Weather. 6.0 News. 6.30 Frank Muir Goes Into . . . domestic Animals. 7.0 News. 7.5 The Archers. 7.20 File on 4. 8.0 Medicine Now. Geoff Watts reports on the health of medical care. 8.30 Making Noise About Life: an American anthropologist working in Morocco. 9.0 In Touch. 9.30 A Sideways Look at . . . 9.45 Kaleidoscope. 10.15 A Bonk at Bedtime.

*Halifax Evening Courier*

SCOTTISH Tories yesterday rejected evolution by a massive majority at their annual conference.

The result delighted party leaders and effectively puts an end to the internal debate which has raged within Scottish Tory ranks since their general election disaster last June.

*Independent*

**7.30 EBONY:** Magazine programme for Britain's black communitues. Reports this week from Chicago about the black haircare industry and from Majorca where a new company is trying to attract more black terrorists to Europe's major resorts.

*Belfast Telegraph*

Naval elements of Iran's Revolutionary Guard equipped with high speed lunches are based on the nearby island of Larak, now Iran's main oil terminal.

*The Observer*

LEYTON Liberal Democrat Jonathon Fryer has been commissioned to write a book on George Fox, founder of the Quackers.

*Waltham Forest Express*

Dirk the talking dog: BBC1, 9pm.

**9.00 A Party Election Broadcast.**
By the SDP.
**9.10 News; Scottish News; Weather.**
**9.40 A Last Chance For Liz (R).**

*Glasgow Herald*

BAG TO BE USED IN CASE OF SICKNESS OR TO GATHER REMAINS.

*Spanish airline sick bag*

# CORRECTION

**DUE to a printing error, a story in last week's Gazette referred to athletics coach Billy Hodgins as an "old waster". This should, of course, have read "old master". We apologise to Mr Hodgins for any embarrassment this has caused.**

The next year she was chosen to sing two numbers in Set to Music, one of the pioneering Eurovision programmes, and in 1960 she played Alice FitzWarren, the Alderman's daughter, in Turn Again Whittington at the London Palladium, opposite Norman Wisdom's Dick.

The next year she was chosen to sing two numbers in the Eurovision programme Set to Music, and in 1960 she played Alice FitzWarren, the Alderman's daughter, in Turn Again Whittington at the London Palladium, with Norman Wisdom playing Dick Whittington.

*Obituary for Yana, Daily Telegraph*
*1st and 2nd editions*

## MAGGIE SOLD!

An autographed photo of Margaret Thatcher fetched £1.60 at a school auction sale in Oyne, Aberdeenshire. A box of haddock raised £8.

*Sunday Mail*

## ABOUT THE AUTHORS

Husband and wife team Ann and Ian Morrison were teenagers in the 1960s and very much part of the era. Ian is well-known for his sports books for Guinness and Hamlyn. Ann has written children's books.

*Breedon Books*

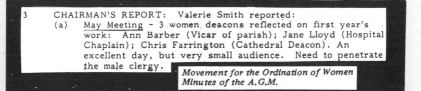

3   CHAIRMAN'S REPORT: Valerie Smith reported:
(a)   May Meeting - 3 women deacons reflected on first year's work: Ann Barber (Vicar of parish); Jane Lloyd (Hospital Chaplain); Chris Farrington (Cathedral Deacon). An excellent day, but very small audience. Need to penetrate the male clergy.

*Movement for the Ordination of Women*
*Minutes of the A.G.M.*

Potentially the greatest bene-fits, however, are the least visible ones. Under the country struc-ture, the territories that were most successful tended to be the ones that expanded the most, while those where penetration was lower stayed small.

*Report on Tambrands (makes of Tampax) in Independent Business Section*

Almost nothing is known of JOHN MAJOR, not even his dates, and even the catalogue of Gooch and Thatcher treats him as no more than a marginal figure.

*Sleeve notes — Shakespearean Songs*

He denied the promotion was as a result of the affair.
"I put her through a series of on-the-job tests to see if she was suitable

*Daily Telegraph*

Mr Perot would not reveal de-tails of his campaign strategy, "but it's going to be serious, you can bet on it, and concen-trated on the issues." His senior adviser, Orson Swindle, said that Mr Perot had prepared a national media blitz and was prepared to spend "tens of mil-lions of dollars to ensure that his message is heard."

*Grauniad*

# Take that!

A BUNGLING thief was feeling fed up yesterday after snatching a bag from Bristol shop manager John Pibworth thinking it was the day's takings. He discovered the bag contained John's supper, a pound of liver and village children."

*Sunday Express*

THE judge in the IRA Bomb trial is feared to be high on the terrorists' hit list. Now 67-year-old Mr. Justice Boreham could face months under the armed round-the-cock protection of Special Branch.

*Belfast Telegraph*

# PRACTICAL EXAMPLE

*BLUE PETER* has no plans to get rid of pregnant presenter Janet Ellis, who is due to produce an unmarried baby in August.

*The Nottingham Evening Post*

Cast members from "Le Nozze di Figaro" at the Glyndebourne Festival Opera in Britain.

*New York Times*

**THE NEW** road initiatives follow a head-on crash between a car and lorry on a double bed at Hembury Fort, near Honiton, which left a North Devon man with serious chest injuries.

*Exeter Express & Star*

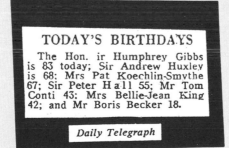

## TODAY'S BIRTHDAYS

The Hon. ir Humphrey Gibbs is 83 today; Sir Andrew Huxley is 68; Mrs Pat Koechlin-Smythe 67; Sir Peter Hall 55; Mr Tom Conti 43; Mrs Bellie-Jean King 42; and Mr Boris Becker 18.

*Daily Telegraph*

Mr Harry Eccleston, OBE, speaks at the opening of the Royal Society of Painters-Etchers and Engravers autumn exhibition, which features a special display of prints by 11 New Zealand printmakers.
Mr Eccleston is president of the society and at night is Mrs Neil Walter, wife of the acting NZ High Commissioner in London,

*TNT Magazine*

Regionally, however, there are differences. This Malaise Anglaise strikes strongest in the Midlands, with Scotland and the North—legendary home of muck 'n bras and hard graft—running second.

*Sunday Express*

All attempts by Labour leader Neil Kinnock and his colleague to prise information from her were met by the same formula repeated *ad nauseam.*
cfi.—u'ty'S—Eifw,Iua.o

*Financial Times*

12 0 IT'S IN THE CLOSET, IT'S UNDER THE BED. A documentary about vampires, werewolves, and other such favourite screen creepies.
12 25 NIGHT THOUGHTS with the Rev Dr Kenneth Wolfe. Close.

*Grauniad*

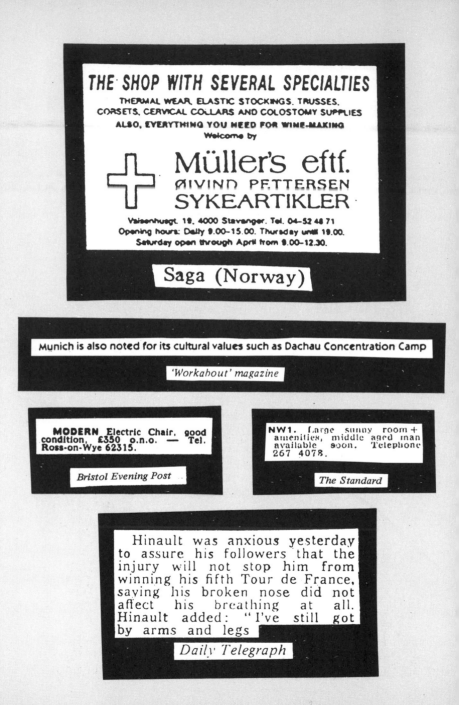

**THE SHOP WITH SEVERAL SPECIALTIES**

THERMAL WEAR, ELASTIC STOCKINGS, TRUSSES,
CORSETS, CERVICAL COLLARS AND COLOSTOMY SUPPLIES

ALSO, EVERYTHING YOU NEED FOR WINE-MAKING

Welcome by

## Müller's eftf.
ØIVIND PETTERSEN
SYKEARTIKLER

Vaisenhusgt. 19, 4000 Stavanger. Tel. 04-52 48 71
Opening hours: Daily 9.00-15.00. Thursday until 19.00.
Saturday open through April from 9.00-12.30.

Saga (Norway)

Munich is also noted for its cultural values such as Dachau Concentration Camp

*'Workabout' magazine*

**MODERN** Electric Chair, good
condition, £350 o.n.o. — Tel.
Ross-on-Wye 62315.

*Bristol Evening Post*

NW1. Large sunny room +
amenities, middle aged man
available soon. Telephone
267 4078.

*The Standard*

Hinault was anxious yesterday
to assure his followers that the
injury will not stop him from
winning his fifth Tour de France,
saying his broken nose did not
affect his breathing at all.
Hinault added: "I've still got
by arms and legs

*Daily Telegraph*

Tynedale Council, which was organising the event, advised that the river was "unsuitable" for bathing due to bacteria including food poisoning orgasms, in the water.

*Newcastle Journal*

Michael Grade, who has a headline on his hips almost as often as a cigar, described yesterday as an "historic" day for the BBC.

*The Times*

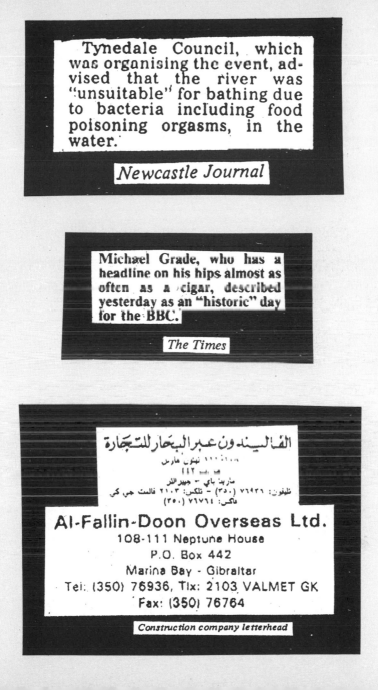

الفـا لـسيند ون عـبر البحار للتجارة

**Al-Fallin-Doon Overseas Ltd.**
108-111 Neptune House
P.O. Box 442
Marina Bay - Gibraltar
Tel: (350) 76936, Tlx: 2103 VALMET GK
Fax: (350) 76764

*Construction company letterhead*

*Gutter pair*

*Stanley Gibbons*

# Illiteracy is still a poblem among Mississippi adults

*Hendersonville Times-News (USA)*

**MAN SHOT DEAD BY POLICE STATION**

*Evening Standard*

## Court out

CAMBRIDGE Crown Court will be closed this week for decorating work to be carried.

All the rooms of the court, excluding the court room and the robbing room, are being painted.

*Cambridge Evening News*

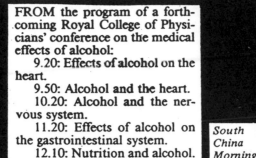

FROM the program of a forth-coming Royal College of Physicians' conference on the medical effects of alcohol:

9.20: Effects of alcohol on the heart.

9.50: Alcohol and the heart.

10.20: Alcohol and the nervous system.

11.20: Effects of alcohol on the gastrointestinal system.

12.10: Nutrition and alcohol.

12.40: Bar open.

*South China Morning Post*

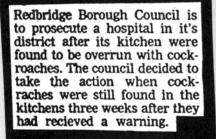

Redbridge Borough Council is to prosecute a hospital in it's district after its kitchen were found to be overrun with cockroaches. The council decided to take the action when cockraches were still found in the kitchens three weeks after they had recieved a warning.

*The Grauniad*

# CRISIS

THE crisis in Sri Lanka epitomises a sad fact that anarchial rule and lawlessness could wreck the orderly government of an emerging third-world country. Such farticidal acts should be avoided.

ALNASHIR D. WALJI,
Nairobi.

*The Standard, Nairobi*

GRANTS OF ST JAMES'S LIMITED

*Established 1700*

WINE MERCHANTS

*Roy Hattersley*

*Sales Representative, Wholesale Division*

*Trade card*

# Helping disabled

DON Castle-Smith has single handedly set up a club to help people come to terms with losing a limb.

*Waltham Forest Express*

Buggers may lurk in the basement of the government's new conference centre

*New Statesman*

All money has now been gathered in from the annual Christmas Carol Concert in Bexley Borough, and the tremendous sum of almost £3,000 has been raised, which will not be distributed amongst various children's charities.

*The Independent*

**AUSTIN ALLEGRO 1300.** Taxed, MoT, radio, £395 ono. Btn. 776155 after 6pm.
**AUSTIN**-Cyril. Forever in our thoughts, Ivy, Jim & family.
**AUSTIN PRINCESS** 2000 HL, 1979. Superb, low mileage, history. £1,095. 673620.

*The London Evening Standard*

Seventeen football supporters, 10 English and seven German, were arrested and a policeman was injured in Dusseldorf last night before West Germany beat England 3-1. Mr Colin Moynihan, Minister for Sport, said he was delighted with the way it had gone.

*The Times*

*The Institute of Cost and Management Accountants*

| Tuesday 27 Jan.1987 7.30 p.m. | Developments in Company Fraud Detective Inspector Wraight, Metropolitan Police Company Fraud Department Venue - Guinness Social Club, Park Royal, N.W.10 |
| --- | --- |

*Harrow and District Branch Programme*

## TALES FROM UGANDA

Councillor Fred Thompson is willing to give a full illustrated talk on his recent visit to Uganda to any interested local clubs or societies.

Fred was a recent guest speaker at Sprotbrough Womens Institute where his talk was well received.

Sprotbrough Parish News

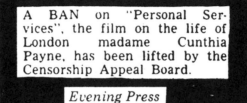

A BAN on "Personal Services", the film on the life of London madame Cunthia Payne, has been lifted by the Censorship Appeal Board.

*Evening Press*

# Guardian fails to appear

### By Staff Reporters

*The Guardian* newspaper did not appear today because of a pay dispute involving members of the Sogat '82 union.

Mr Ian Wright, managing editor said tat production was halted when fewer than 20 London-based messengers refused to end a meeting.

*The Times*

# SAVE ILEA PUBLIC MEETING

Are you interested in your children's education?

What happens if the threatened abolition of ILEA is carried out?

What effect it will have on:

1   General Scool education

2   Youth Services

3   Adult education

4   Access and second chance courses

5   Nursery education and other aspects

If ILEA is abolished can the London Bouroughs continue to maintain the existing standards?  How will the rates be affected?

Come and discuss these maters at a

# PUBLIC MEETING

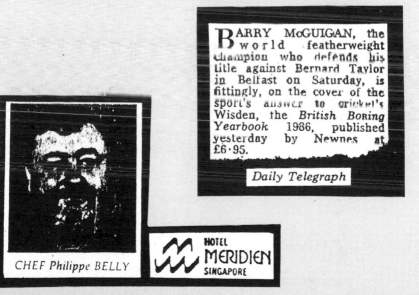

**B**ARRY McGUIGAN, the world featherweight champion who defends his title against Bernard Taylor in Belfast on Saturday, is fittingly, on the cover of the sport's answer to cricket's Wisden, the *British Boxing Yearbook* 1986, published yesterday by Newnes at £6·95.

*Daily Telegraph*

CHEF Philippe BELLY

HOTEL
MERIDIEN
SINGAPORE

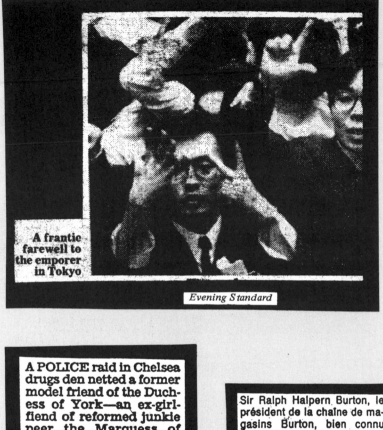

**A frantic farewell to the emporer in Tokyo**

*Evening Standard*

A POLICE raid in Chelsea drugs den netted a former model friend of the Duchess of York—an ex-girlfiend of reformed junkie peer the Marquess of Blandford, son of the Duke of Marlborough—a court was told today.

*Evening Standard*

Sir Ralph Halpern Burton, le président de la chaîne de magasins Burton, bien connu pour sa rigueur morale, retire de la vente tous les vêtements portant l'image de Smiley.

*Le Figaro*

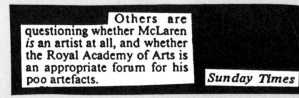

Others are questioning whether McLaren *is* an artist at all, and whether the Royal Academy of Arts is an appropriate forum for his poo artefacts.

*Sunday Times*

And a Nightingale Sang (ITV) was like a stretched Hovis ad with some real acting. Set in Newcastle during the war, it had a bravura performance by Phyllis Logan as Helen, a lovely innocent lass who falls for a squaddie (Tom Watt) whose compassionate manner conceals a belief that love is ultimately just a passing fanny.

*Observer*

## A royal grandson

LONDON, Friday: British Prime Minister Margaret Thatcher has become a grandmother.

*Syndey Morning Herald*

# Writer acquitted

FAMOUS Ham gossip columnist Nigel Dempster was acquitted of a drink driving charge this week because of his fear of needles.

*Surrey Comet*

# Smog Threatens Iran

Pollution could make Tehran inhabitable within about 30 years unless urgent measures are taken, acting Mayor Mohammed Hossein Tabatabei said last week.

*Middle East Times*

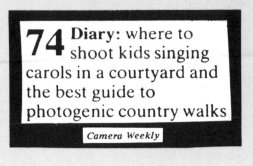

**74** **Diary:** where to shoot kids singing carols in a courtyard and the best guide to photogenic country walks

*Camera Weekly*

**FUND RAISING OFFICER**
**SCHOTTISH COUNCIL ON ALCOIIOL (S.C.A.(**

*Glasgow Herald*

BRIGADIER Ronnie Stonham, the man in room 105 at Broadcasting House alleged to vet BBC staff for the security services, is not an MI5 van, staff were told yesterday.

*Grauniad*

NOVELIST Graham Greene intervened publicly yesterday in conflict within the financially-troubled publishing group of Chatto, Virago, Bodley Head and Jonathan ape.

*The Observer*

**SMITH CORONA™**

Introducing The Spell-Right III™ Electronic Dicitionary

*South China Morning Post*

# APOLOGY

In the edition of the Sunday Press dated March 18, 1990 in this column a photograph of Proinsias De Rossa T.D., M.E.P., was published with the caption underneath the said photograph reading "prospective monster?" This caption should have read "prospective Minister?" We apologise to Mr. De Rossa for the false implication arising from this error and for the embarrassment and inconvenience caused to him.

*Please contact Tony Aylward, Human Resources, Chevron UK Ltd., 2 Portman Street, London W1H 0AN. Tel: 01-487-8911.*

*Chevron welcomes sex with all suitably disabled people regardless of size of bank balance.*

*Chevron Advertisement, Evening Standard*

**THE INSOLVENCY ACT 1986
IN BANKRUPTCY
IN THE BRIGHTON
COUNTY COURT
No. 80 of 1990**

Re: Michael Pearson of 4 Bloomsbury Street, Kemp Town, Brighton BN2 1HQ Satellite Television Dish Installer also formerly known as Pratt

**Explore France on a Horse!**
Village Gits.
Self Catering or Full Board.

*Horse & Pony*

**5.20 THE CLOT SHOW:**
Fashion programme this week features a glimpse inside the wardrobes of the late Duchess of Windsor, and the Fabric of the Nation exhibition in Edinburgh.

*Today*

**TELEPHONE EXTENSION** socket kit, 30 metres £8. Small electric organ, good for learning £30ono. Also large orgasm.

*Wandsworth Times*

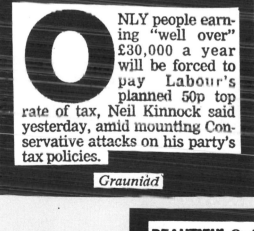

NLY people earning "well over" £30,000 a year will be forced to pay Labour's planned 50p top rate of tax, Neil Kinnock said yesterday, amid mounting Conservative attacks on his party's tax policies.

*Grauniad*

**BEAUTIFUL** Swiss widow, fifties, seeks self made man. I'm 169, blond, cheerful, healthy, non-smoker, honest, tender, financially secure, experienced hostess.

*The Times*

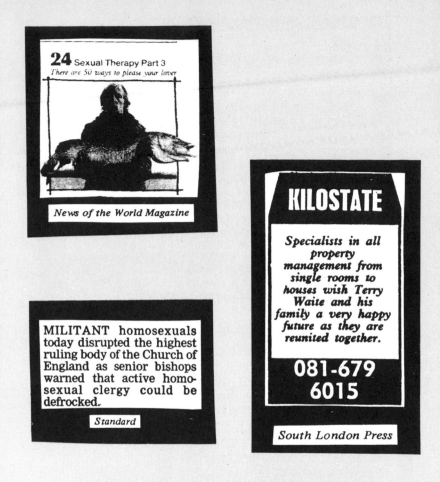

**24** Sexual Therapy Part 3
*There are 50 ways to please your lover*

*News of the World Magazine*

# KILOSTATE

*Specialists in all property management from single rooms to houses wish Terry Waite and his family a very happy future as they are reunited together.*

**081-679 6015**

*South London Press*

MILITANT homosexuals today disrupted the highest ruling body of the Church of England as senior bishops warned that active homosexual clergy could be defrocked.

*Standard*

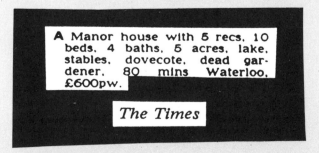

**A** Manor house with 5 recs, 10 beds, 4 baths, 5 acres, lake, stables, dovecote, dead gardener, 80 mins Waterloo, £600pw.

*The Times*

# On the catwalk ——————

Members of Shaftesbury Boys Club modelling the latest fashions at the launch of the club's refurbishment appeal.

Foot tasting, arranged through the courtesy of Marks & Spencers and Safeway, gives customers a rare chance to try some of those more exotic flavours.

*Nags Head Shopping Centre advertisement*

**BINOCULARS** 16x50 field 3.s sirius coated lens with case, hardly used after 6 o'clock, £15.—

*Sevenoaks Chronicle*

The "Candidates on Television" listing yesterday misspelled the name of the Vice President in some editions. It is Quayle, not Quale. The Tmise regrets the error.

*New York Times*

# In the  home

# Ethnic cleansing: You and your shower unit

*Jersey Evening Post*

It says it got the side-on colour picture of the duchess with one breast exposed, along with three others inside, from the European TV magazine Cine Tele Revue.

*Oxford Mail*

Die Serie moderner Sex-Skandale, an die sich die Briten gerne erinnern, begann in den permissiven sechziger Jahren mit der Profumo-Affäre. Dem Verteidigungsminister Harold Macmillan folgten Lord Lambton und die Thatcher-Günstlinge Devil Parkinson und Jeffrey Archer.

 *Die Zeit*

INVALID chair, 'Dudly Extra plus Electronic' complete with lights, indicators and safety belt, has substantial kerb-crawling facility, necessary batteries and battery charger, excellent condition, paid £1,900, for sale at £1,199 o.n.o. —

*Harrogate Champion Shopper*

**Baby joy on a special weekend for all mums**

# HAPPY GRAN'S DAY

## Maggie thrilled by news of her first grandson

*Daily Mirror*

## Mr. Ted Jackson

In our story on the history of Kingstonian Ices, Mr. Ted Jackson was incorrectly reported as describing the container in which the ice cream was sold as being shaped like a urine glass. It should have been a wine glass. We are sorry for any embarrassment this may have caused.

*Surrey Comet*

**FOUR UK** 5.55 Shipping. 6.0 News; Weather. 6.10 Farting. 6.25 Prayer. 6.30 Today. 8.35 Yesterday in Parlia-

*Liverpool Daily Post*

It would be a great help if Wykehamists kept the Keeper Informed of interesting appointments, or deaths of themselves or their friends. The address is: The Keeper of Wykehamist Records, The College, Winchester SO23 9LX.

The Reserves League Cup Semi-final match was postponed due to the already played other semi final containing illegible players.

*All Sport Weekly*

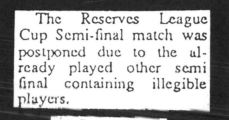

Ian specialises in coaching those with little musical skill and works closely with the likes of Hal Prince, Andrew Lloyd Webber, Adam Faith, Bonnie Langford and Sarah Brightman.

*Southern Evening Echo*

## Community Charge Registration Form

Community Charge Registration Officer for your area: Lindsay Robb, IPFA
CANVASS REMINDER

The Occupier

PUBLIC CONVENIENCE
FRONT 241 KING STREET

Property Reference

The children confide in the passenger on the train, who tells them he followed the trail and thinks their father is innocent. As this filf is directed by Lionel Jeffries it must have a happy ending.

*Barking and Dagenham Advertiser*

*Bristol Evening Post*

*U.K. Press Gazette*

PRESS ASSOCIATION NEWS AT 4PM

...MRS THATCHER HAS DEFENDED U.S. ATTACKS ON LIBYA AS ''WITHIN THEIR INHERENT RIGHT OF SELF ABUSE.... THAT WAS WHY WE GAVE OUR SUPPORT AND OUR CONSENT TO THE USE OF BASES IN BRITAIN FOR THAT PURPOSE.''

QUEEN ELIZABETH 11,
HEAD OF COMMONWEALTH

*Monrovia Daily Star, Liberia*

# Surma Tandoori Restaurant

### *Where East Meets West*

Dine in style and enjoy superb Indian and Tandoori cuisine at Bedford's Premier Indian Restaurant
* Full licensed * Full take-away service
* Authentic Indian Doctor

*Bedford Herald*

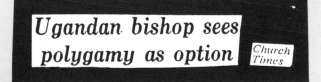

*Ugandan bishop sees polygamy as option*

*Church Times*

A village vet in Spain turned his horse upside-down in a frantic search for a missing lottery ticket while villagers waited outside for news.

*Daily Telegraph*

About 160 people attended the show A 'psychic team' passed massages from the dead to members of the audience.

*Blackburn Citizen*

Gob Geldof, caballero del imperio británico

Aylsham's Plant Aid stall made the grand total of £0. The organisers thank all concerned.

*Norfolk Advertiser*

## A ringing call

A NEW team of bell ringers is being formed at St Margaret's Church, West Hoathly.

Both experienced and novice bell ringers interested in joining the group are invited to the church on Monday, September 22, at 8pm when experienced bell ringer, Ian Harris, will get the group off the ground.

*Mid Sussex Times*

**7.00**
**Film:**
ET the Extra-Terrestrial

*The Independent*

**Deaths**           *Veterinary Record*

**Dr P. J. Posthumus**

R. G. M. writes — Dr Peter Jacobus
Posthumus, who died in August 1991,

MOUSSAKA is a traditional
Greek dish that incorporates
aubergines, meat and potatoes
in a smooth shite sauce.
It takes a long time to prepare,
and if you are a moussaka fan

*Ilford & Redbridge Post*

**GCHQ** plays a vital role in protecting
the security of the nation's official and
military communications. Each year
we select a small number of the
brighest graduates to join the special
Graduate Management Training
Scheme. Degree discipline is less
important than the interlectual calibre
and the potential of an individual to
develop into our senior managers of
the future.

*Careers Guide*

대영여행사
Dai Young Travel

*Korean Weekly*

# NEW INSTRUCTIONS AT REDUCED PRICE

## LEDBURY

A modern house of attractive mock Tudor design situated on the popular Robinson Meadow development within wanking distance of the town centre. The property provides well presented, gas centrally heated accommodation which comprises: ENTRANCE HALL, SITTING ROOM, FITTED KITCHEN, DINING ROOM, THREE BEDROOMS, BATHROOM. The house stands in an area of lawned garden with parking to the front.

### £59,000

*Malvern Gazette*

If the weather is good the Regiment's freefall parachute team, the Flying Dragons, will land five of its members on the lawn. This will be followed by beating the recruit.

*Tonbridge News*

Shortly afterwards Mr Peet — then a young curate — met him in a homosexual bar. "I used to go there", the vicar admits, "just to be in genial company, relax, be myself. I think today there are more gay organisations, but in those days one was groping in the gloom for comfort and support."

*The Times*

A late 19th century Thatcher Milk Protector.    £150

*A fortune in your attic*

## Apology to nurses

Last week's *NALGO News* reported the general principles involved in the clinical grading appeals for 'horses', midwives and health visitors. This, of course, should have read 'nurses'. Our apologies for any offence or embarrassment this typographical error may have caused.

Due to ever increasing business in our restaurant and banqueting department, we require several staff to join our small friendly team.

No previous experience is necessary, as full training will be given.

The shits are on a rota basis and can be flexible to suit.

If you have any number of evenings free and would like further details.

**Contact: KAREN — 604128**

*Garstang Courier*

Likewise, Eileen Reid is a real discovery . . . again. She shows a real fleshy *feel* for the part of Rosie the prostitute (as David Herlihy will, no doubt, confirm) and on opening night she received the clap she so richly deserved.

*Sunday Independent*

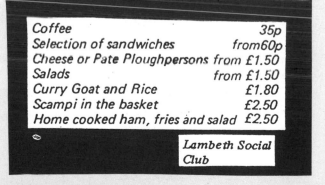

| | |
|---|---|
| Coffee | 35p |
| Selection of sandwiches | from 60p |
| Cheese or Pate Ploughpersons | from £1.50 |
| Salads | from £1.50 |
| Curry Goat and Rice | £1.80 |
| Scampi in the basket | £2.50 |
| Home cooked ham, fries and salad | £2.50 |

*Lambeth Social Club*

**SENIOR STAFF NURSE — Grade E**
**JUNIOR SISTER — Grade F**
**RGN'S — EN'S**
**RGN's — EN'S — BANK NURSES**

Due to our continued success within the local community, we require these posts for our lousy surgical and medical wards.

*RODING HOSPITAL*

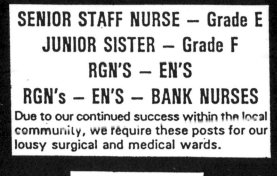

Mr Ronald Brown (Edinburgh, Leith, Lab) said that the Government had been complacent too long. Floating voters would expect coastal waters to at least meet the standard of the average European country,

*The Times*

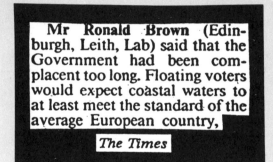

## OOPS! SORRY!

*The story carried last week entitled 'Lesbian nurses tear legs apart' was accidentally accredited to Pete Sankey. We apologise for this error.*

*The Weekend Enquirer (Jamaica)*

A spokesman for the Water Authorities Association claimed yesterday that there would be no charge for free water after the sell-off.

*Grauniad*

Then, as a result of finding a small amount of cannabis in his pocket, they searched his home in Eason View, Dringhouses, where they found bed linen and towels hidden in a bin liner.

*Yorkshire Evening Press*

**10.00 ST ELSEWHERE.** One of Morrison's patients has an incurable disease. Morrison must tell him the bad news. With David Morse.

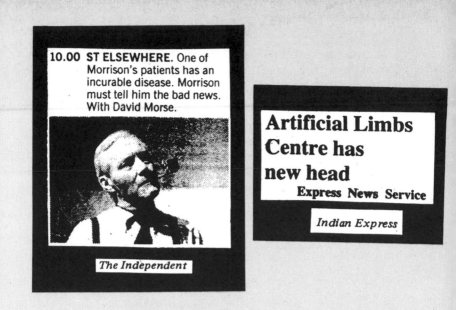

*The Independent*

# Artificial Limbs Centre has new head

**Express News Service**

*Indian Express*

Transport Minister Robert Atkins opened the sale and was pissed when he said he hoped bidders would pay a lot for the plates because the money was going to the taxpayers.

*China Post*

And that is certainly true for the Birling family in J.B. Priestley's modern classic An Inspector Calls which is being revived at Bromley's Churchill Theatre.

Alfred Marks lays the officer of the title, although in this clever mystery his character has hidden depths.

*Caterham Comet Leader*

■ Due to a transcription error, an article in Saturday's *Independent* on page 2 on Irish premier Charles Haughey mistakenly read "a man of immense rudeness". This was intended to read "a man of great shrewdness".

*The Independent*

# Condom is back in French pack

*The Independent*

Readers will recall in particular the Lockheed Problem leading to a former LDP prime minister convicted of trousering a £2-million bride being sentenced to four years in prison

*Spectator*

On Saturday, Muslim fundamentalists burned tyres and hurled stones in Bethlehem, prompting border police to close shops and clear the streets of everyone except tourists.

*Jordan Times*

The World seems to have forgotten them in their misery. There is still some aid coming in. Geoffrey Archer, the famous novelist, adventurer, parliamentarian and philanderer was in the region last week bringing welcome aid from Great Britain.

*Briefing Ankara*

"I realised that he had been lying, cold, so cold and cruel. I just felt I was going to pieces.'

## Major's wife given psychiatric care for killing

*Grauniad*

# Names of town, district council chairmen and their vices released

*Malawi Daily Times*

Tomorrow the head keeper of an estate in Islay appears at Campbeltown Sheriff Court charged with laying a hen's egg spiked with alphachloralose.

*Aberdeen Press & Journal*

● The race is won — British Telecom's 'Royal Ascot' float which won the Cornish float championship prize.

*The West Briton & Royal Cornwall Gazette*

# Anniversary Dinner

Among the special guests attending the Brecon Rotary Club's 30th Charter Anniversary dinner but not included in the report in our last week's issue was the President of the Brecon Soroptimist Club and not the President of the United States of America as inadvertentlly appeared. We apologise for any embarrassment to the organisers or the invited guests which this error may have caused.

*Brecon & Radnor Express*

# Sorry!

THE "Peeblesshire News" would like to apologise for any embarrassment caused by last week's typographical error in the Sheriff Court report headed "Two assaults." The words "dirty book" should have read "dirty look."

**WEATHER**

Dry. Some shunshine.
Details — Back Page

*Daily Telegraph*

**The Dail Mail** takes no responsibility for any inaccuracy in an advertisement

*Daily Mail*

# Jumping in at the deep end of life

UNDISCOVERED ENDS by Bruce Kent
(Harper Collins, £15.95)

HE will have no memory of it, but once, in a down
moment, I had the good fortune to meet Bruce Kent
when he was parish priest of St Aloysius, the round
Euston Station. His response then w...

# Seeing the other side of Maxwell

MAXWELL STORIES by Sam Jaffa
(Robson Books, £8.99)

EVERYONE has a Maxwell story. Some of the best I
heard while working in Fleet Street – and some I
didn't – are collected in Sam Jaffa's book.
Jaffa is not the first to write a book about Cap'n
– to the man...

*The Universe*

**7.30 AIRWAVES.** Every-one has something to hide. In Alex's case it's a gambling obesssion. Bobby lends some much-needed advice. Stars Robert Maxwell, Ingrid Veninger

*The Sun*

The European is thought to be losing about £1 million a week, although Mr Maxwell said that it and the Daily News were "doing very well". He repeated his assertion mad earlier this year that both papers were "in danger of making a profit in their first year of existence".

*Grauniad*

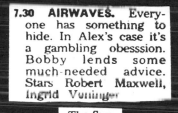

5. Kevin manufactures ocean going yachts to customer specifications. Work on the most recent job has just been completed at a cost of £120,000. However, Kevin has just received a letter from the customer's solicitor informing him that the customer has drowned in a boating accident, and, as his executor he has decided not to proceed with the purchase of the yacht even though this means forfeiting the £30,000 deposit. Under the agreement, Kevin is not entitled to any further money from the customer's estate. Fortunately a new customer, Jackson, is interested in purchasing. Kevin must decide whether to sell the yacht in its existing state to Max's Motor Cruisers for £5,000 or to carry out modifications to meet Jackson's requirements. Jackson would require the work to be carried out within 6 weeks. Kevin's office manager has prepared a schedule to help establishing the price to be charged to Jackson as follows:

|  | £ | £ |
|---|---|---|
| Costs to date |  | 120,000 |
| less non-returnable deposit |  | 30,000 |
|  |  | 90,000 |

*Acountancy exam paper*

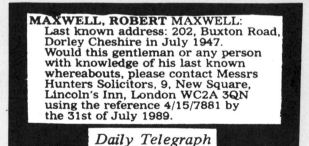

MAXWELL, ROBERT MAXWELL:
Last known address: 202, Buxton Road, Dorley Cheshire in July 1947.
Would this gentleman or any person with knowledge of his last known whereabouts, please contact Messrs Hunters Solicitors, 9, New Square, Lincoln's Inn, London WC2A 3QN using the reference 4/15/7881 by the 31st of July 1989.

*Daily Telegraph*

# HOW TO LIVE

ON

# A SHILLING A WEEK

London:

JOHN & ROBERT MAXWELL

MILTON HOUSE, SHOE LANE, FLEET STREET

AND

35, ST. BRIDE STREET, LUDGATE CIRCUS, E.C.

*Title page*

**Maxwell as Verdi's Falstaff, complete with shimmering latex belly.**

*The Independent*

*Maxwell Montes. Maxwell covers an area larger than Washington and Oregon, and stands almost 7 miles above the mean planetary radius. Maxwell's western slopes are very steep, while it descends gradually into the highlands of Fortuna Tessera on the east. Linear pull-apart features cover much of Maxwell's western half. Cleopatra is just to the right of center.*

**Mercury – The Journal of the Astronomical Society of the Pacific**

# HOW TO PUT ON FLESH.

## WITH SPECIAL INSTRUCTIONS AS TO DIET AND EXERCISE.

Illustrated.

BY

"UNCLE BOB."

HEALTH AND STRENGTH,
12 Burleigh Street, Strand, W.C.

*Title Page*

**Un'edicola a Budapest e,** a sinistra, **Rupert Murdoch con una copia del suo nuovo giornale europeo. L' editore inglese ha investito massicciamente in Ungheria**

*La Republica*

THE OPEAN

Maxwell then named himself chairman, saying he hoped that would lead to the company's future growth.

*Electronic Engineering Times*

His last voyage was to the coast of Guinea. He had been on board a slave ship, the captain's name Maxwell, where one man had been killed, a boy put to lodge with the pigs and was half eaten, one boy set to watch in the hot sun till he dropped down dead. He had been cast away in North America and had travelled thirty days among the Indians, where he had been well treated. He had twice swum from a King's ship in the night and escaped. He said he would rather be in hell than be pressed. He was now going to wait in England to appear against Captain Maxwell. 'O he's a Rascal, Sir, he ought to be put in the papers!'

*Dorothy Wordsworth's "Journal" of 1802*

# MARKETING WEEK

MAY 3, 1991 £1.40
VOLUME 14 No 8

**COVER**

FLOATING ISSUE:
HOW SHIPSHAPE
ARE MAXWELL'S
NEWSPAPERS?

**PITCHER**

The nine-carat truth
about Gerald Ratner's
candid revelation

**ANALYSIS**

Pressure at the pump:
Why regional brewers
are feeling the pinch

**PROFILE**

Carl Tiflin built a high fire in the fire-place and told stories. He told about the wild man who ran naked through the country and had a tail and ears like a horse, and he told about the rabbit-cats of Moro Cojo that hopped into the trees for birds. He revived the famous Maxwell brothers who found a vein of gold and hid the traces of it so carefully that they could never find it again.

*From 'The Red Pony' by John Steinbeck (1939)*

ROBERT MAXWELL

*EMI record sleeve (1960)*

HIS HARPS AND HIS ORCHESTRA

# SPECTACULAR HARPS

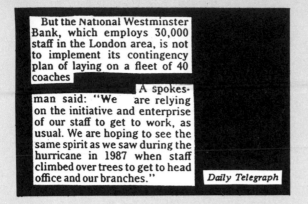

But the National Westminster Bank, which employs 30,000 staff in the London area, is not to implement its contingency plan of laying on a fleet of 40 coaches

A spokesman said: "We are relying on the initiative and enterprise of our staff to get to work, as usual. We are hoping to see the same spirit as we saw during the hurricane in 1987 when staff climbed over trees to get to head office and our branches."

*Daily Telegraph*

"With the dissent in the control room, we did bring in union representation from the operational crews. However, there are 39 crews on duty during the day, and it represented one operations person being deployed per shit. This temporary measure is due to end next week."

*Leatherhead Advertiser*

Chiu Mei Au Yeung, who works for VNU's *Computer Business Week*, was particularly thrilled as the holiday will give her an opportunity to sell her Hong-Kong based family, whom she has not seen for many years.

*Magazine Week*

Homes, shops and offices evacuated over wide area of Bermondsey after workmen found 500lb unexploded wartime bomb. Bomb found on building site at Mill Street, near Tower Bridge. Workmen thought object was old pope and tried to break casing with excavator.

*Evening Standard*

## Lamont Financial Services

**Investment, Pension and Finance Specialists**
Century House, 298-302 London Road, Sheffield S2 4NA UK   Telephone: (0742) 500181

(FIMBRA)
MEMBER

Partners: D. M. Blogg, M. B. Lamb, J. Pickering
Member of the Financial Intermediaries, Managers and Brokers Regulatory Association

# Trial for Andreotti?

Yet, events in the past couple of days have shown a remarkable shit, not only against him, but against the system he symbolized.

*News International, Pakistan*

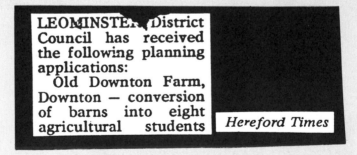

LEOMINSTER District Council has received the following planning applications:
   Old Downton Farm, Downton — conversion of barns into eight agricultural students

*Hereford Times*

DAVID JOHN MELLOR, BA 1970, was given, in the 8th Annual Highland Park/Spectator Parliamentarians of the Year Award, the award of "Member to Watch".

*Christ's College Magazine, 1992*

They are also interested in reminiscences from people who wee in the audience on the last night at any local cinemas or theatres.

*Hull Daily Mail*

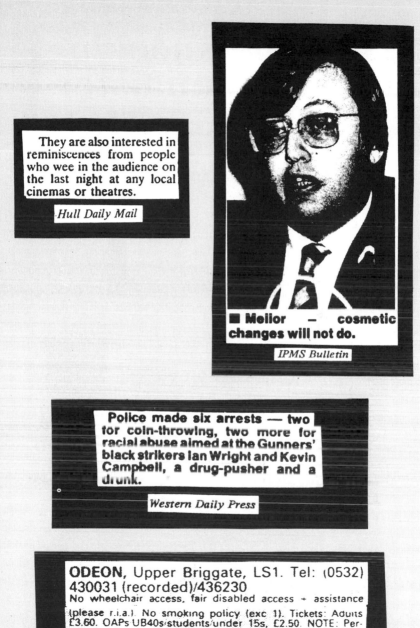

■ Melior — cosmetic changes will not do.

*IPMS Bulletin*

Police made six arrests — two for coin-throwing, two more for racial abuse aimed at the Gunners' black strikers Ian Wright and Kevin Campbell, a drug-pusher and a drunk.

*Western Daily Press*

**ODEON**, Upper Briggate, LS1. Tel: (0532) 430031 (recorded)/436230
No wheelchair access, fair disabled access + assistance (please r.i.a.). No smoking policy (exc 1). Tickets: Adults £3.60. OAPs UB40s/students/under 15s, £2.50. NOTE: Persons in wheelchairs - free admission

# Stop the knocking says fun minister

*Morning Advertiser*

## Jehovah's Witnesses

9 Brandon Road, Stanley
Telephone: 21267
Secretary - Mr A A Nutter

**TV STAR SUPPORTS COMPANY**
Judith Chalmers, TV celebrity, has lent her support to Safe-Buy UK

*Redbridge Guardian*

The only change England would propose might be to replace Derek Pringle, who remains troubled by no-balls,

*The Times*

## Doctors 'very concerned' about Mother Teresa

*Independent*

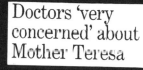

## Personal 1

**S. PARASKOS** and Helen Walker would like to announce that they are no longer engaged.

**ENGAGEMENT** S. Paraskos of Paphos, Cyprus and Nicola Jared of UK would like to announce their engagement.

*Cyprus Weekly*

The women's unit has boasted of its work with the Proud Old Lesbians, the Irish Lesbian Network and the Turkish Lesbian Group. Conservative opposition leader Joe Lobenstein says: "I'm all in favour of race equality but this is just jobs for the boys.

*Evening Standard*

THE Hereford branch of Arthritis Care would like to thank all the people who turned out to their coffee morning on Thursday, December 12, despite the bitterly cold weather.

We were particularly pleased that the Mayor and Mayoress, Councillor and Mrs Turbutt, were unable to attend.

Anyone who does not apply research to the original appreciation of the situation and to the assessment of results is behaving like a blind man with neither a white stick nor a guide dog.

Yet management and clients do put their penises in blind men's begging bowls.

*Frank Jefkins,*
*Principal,*
*Frank Jefkins School of Public Relations*

**2 SANTA CLAUS —THE MOVIE** (U)
At 2.30 p.m.
*A powerful, sinister thriller that'll scare you to your very soul*

And unimaginable. However, explicit language was condemned while sexual activities were condomed by euphemism.

# Asbestos threat

ASBESTOS garages which may have been blown apart in the winds should be kept damp in a plastic bag say environmental health officers.

Within any 7-day period, you can get the local equivalent of US$500 cash and US$500 in American Express® Travelers Cheques and charge it to your Card Account*, at the touch of a bottom. 24 hours a day. 365 days a year.

# Ministers show 'the ugly face of Toryism'

*The Times*

When Prince Charles and Lady Diana Cooper were married in July, 1981, their wedding set a global record: more than a quarter of the world's 4.7 billion population was believed to have followed the royal event on television.

*Northwest Airlines flight magazine*

# Pressure group

In some editions of yesterday's Guardian the pressure group Families for Legal Rights was incorrectly described as Families for Illegal Rights. We regret this error.

*Grauniad*

Plans for a new cricket pavilion at Coppid Hall Cricket Club, Binfield Heath, have been given the go-ahead by district councillors.

Phillimore Settled Estates will demolish the old pavilion and install a septic tank.

*Henley Standard*

*The Herald*

**11.05 — OFF THE PAGE†**
Poet Laureate Ted Rogers introduces five of his poems in a stark and haunting manner.

*South Wales Echo*

Lloyd — a senior executive with Carlton Greeting Cards — was posted to England

*Yorkshire Evening Post*

Borchardt is accused of disturbing the peace by hurling a choir against the window of the Turkish cultural centre, situated next to the right-wingers' local pub, and frequented at the time by a number of intimidated foreigners.

*Grauniad*

**ELVIS** seeks garden work Mon Tues Wed Fri. Has refs. Tel: Edith 7018230.
AG0066

*The Highway Mail, Durban*

**THE HUNGARIAN SOCIAL CLUB**

Members' notice

**ST PATRICK'S DAY DANCE**

**TUES 17 MARCH**

Entertainment by

**THE SHANNON CIDERS TRIO**

# Mrs D Williams

IN reporting in our last issue an Inquest on Flt. Lt. Kenneth Williams, of Collyer Road, Stokenchurch, we suggested that his widow, Dorothy, appeared to be distraught during the hearing. She has asked to make it clear that this was not the case. Our apologies for any embarrassment caused.

*Bucks Free Press*

# 'Animals will suffer if abattoir closes'

*Gravesend Evening Post*

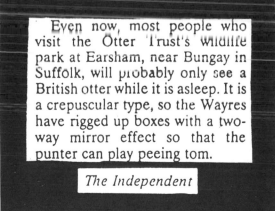

Even now, most people who visit the Otter Trust's wildlife park at Earsham, near Bungay in Suffolk, will probably only see a British otter while it is asleep. It is a crepuscular type, so the Wayres have rigged up boxes with a two-way mirror effect so that the punter can play peeing tom.

*The Independent*

**Lord Mowbray and Stourton:** My Lords, can my noble friend the Minister inform me whether or not this Japanese knotweed is a cousin of our old friend sticky willie, from which I suffer?

*Hansard*

More than a quarter of those questioned are also critical about the number of spelling mistakes and gramatical errors in CVs, as well as their scruffy appearance and sparce detail.

*Daily Telegraph*

He claimed solvent abuse and butane gas inhalation was going on under the noses of residents, who did not realise it.

*Isle of Wight Country Press*

# Court story

WE apologise for placing an incorrect heading on a court story in page 23 of our June 29 issue.

It read " Father headbuts his son" but should have read " Father headbuts his son's attacker".

We are sorry for any offence caused to Jeffrey Babbs of Don Court, Witham.

*Braintree and Witham Times*

# The boys in "green"

West Midlands Police force is going "green" to protect the environment, to the extent of possibly using lead-free bullets.

*Birmingham Choice*

● Thieves took precautions when they snatched a condom and contents, worth £230, from a toilet at the Banbury Cross pub in Butcher's Row, Banbury, last week.

*The Banbury Cake*

## ICE SHIP REFIT

The Navy's 30-year old ice patrol ship Endurance is to have a £15 million refit to keep her in service until the mid-1900s.

*Daily Telegraph*

In paragraph eight we referred to the company as a "*terrible* British company", this should of course have read as "a *terribly* British company".

*Fashion Weekly referring to Hackett menswear*

**MARKS — SPARKES.**
— The wedding of Robert James Marks and Angela Elizabeth Sparkes is taking place at St. Matthews Church, Cainscross. on Saturday 11th October 1986, 12.30 p.m. All friends welcome at the Church.

*Stroud News & Journal*

SEXUAL BODY TALK

SUSAN QUILLIAM

UNDERSTANDING THE BODY LANGUAGE OF ATTRACTION FROM FIRST GLANCE TO SEXUAL HAPPINESS

*Professor John Malins*
*David & Charles 0 7153 9899 7*
*£20.00*
An indispensable companion to all gardeners who wish to create a beautiful garden full of handsome, healthy and productive plants.

*Publishing News*

David Tredinnick with the Prime Minister at No. 10 Downing Street, at a reception to raise money for Huntingdon's disease.

*Election Manifesto*

**HOSPITAL JOB CUTS**

The Royal London has a four million pound defecation has not been able to attract enough patients to cover its high costs.

*The Asian*

A GREY Seal pup, found starving to death in Peel Harbour, has been rescued by the manager of the Curraghs Wildlife Park.

Telephone calls from concerned relatives alerted staff at the Park who discovered the ailing seal close to death.

*The Manx Independent*

**FOR THE BRIDE**

**PERSONAL ATTACK ALARM** Feel Safe, the very best in personal protection. No salesman, no pressure, just the latest technology at prices you'll find hard to beat. For free information call — M. A. Holdings 0623 632681.

*Nottingham Evening Post*

Between 11.00 and 12.30 Friday night some ferretts valued at about £28.00 were stolen from Milton Abbey School. The thief is advised not to put the ferretts in his pockets as they are carnivours

*Stour Valley News*

A Humberside Police spokesman said: "We have been expecting this since it was announced late last year.

*Hull Daily Mail*

Three boys escaped when a wall collapsed at the Zoological Gardens, Regent's Park, London.

*The Times*

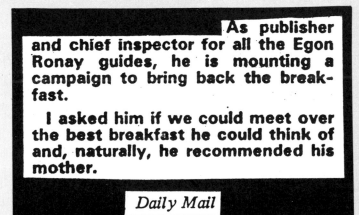

As publisher and chief inspector for all the Egon Ronay guides, he is mounting a campaign to bring back the breakfast.

I asked him if we could meet over the best breakfast he could think of and, naturally, he recommended his mother.

*Daily Mail*

**Mackenzie Stuart,** President of the Court of Justice, European Communities, 64.

Our Barman Recommends

Cocktail Of The Week :

"MID AIR COLLISION"

(white rum, blue curacao, pineapple juice, coconut cream)

**Pretty And Fit Cyclist**—Seeking male Jewish partner, 35-45, to travel highways of life making titstops for marriage and kids. Will take all cultural, intellectual and recreational detours. 9702 ✉

*New York Magazine*

**MATCHES** have hundreds of unattacked people in the Hants, Berks and Surrey areas, aged 17-70, so do join us. — Tel. (0264) 51853, Matches, Dept FN, 19-23 Bridge Street, Andover, Hants.

*Camberley & District Courier*

**From Derek Brown in Bonn**
European governments should combine in research on a new generation of high technology weapons — either by contributing to the US Start Wars project, or to their own independent programme — the German Foreign Minister, Mr Hans-Dietrich Genscher, said yesterday at the start of Western European Union ministerial talks here.

*The Guardian*

George Bush made one of the all-time misstatements Friday night at the College of Southern Idaho. Describing his close relationship with President Reagan, Bush said: "For 7½ years I've worked alongside him, and I'm proud to be his partner. We've had triumphs, we've made mistakes, we've had sex.

"Setbacks," he quickly corrected. "We've had setbacks."

With a little smile, he then told the laughing audience, "I feel like the javelin competitor who won the toss and elected to receive."

*San Francisco Chronicle*

# Grace Darling

PUPILS at Halstead's St Andrew's School were raising money for the Grace Darling Lifeboat and not the Grey Starling as stated last week.

*Halstead Gazette*

I think the Poll Tax is unfair, unjust and democratic

☐ I would like more details about Labour's campaign against it

☐ I am interested in joining the Labour Party

Name

Address

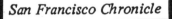

Labour

Please return to: Hornsey and Wood Green Labour Party, Freepost, 28 Middle Lane, London N8

*Melvyn Bragg, 9.45* | *Sunday Mirror*

The first week of November passed in a buzz of activity, as the Annual Day approached nearer. It arrived at last, on the 10th. Ch. Devi Lal, the honourable Chief Minister of Haryana, was the Chief Guest and he presided over the function. The programme went off well without a bitch, and the whole school got a day off on the 11th.

*Rai Times*

Le patron de News International — propriétaire notamment du « Times » et du « Sun » le plus gros titage de la presse britannique —

*Les Echos*

Between February and July last year 125 children were diagnosed as sexually abused — 121 of them by the consultants Dr Marietta Higgs and Dr Geoffrey Wyatt — and 67 became wards of court

*Financial Times*

Despite a 2000 signature petition backed by naturalists Sir Peter Scott, Sir David Attenborough and David Bellamy, 38 wildflowers have secured a five-year lease to shoot hundreds of ducks along the mouth of Camel River, Cornwall.

*Evening Standard*

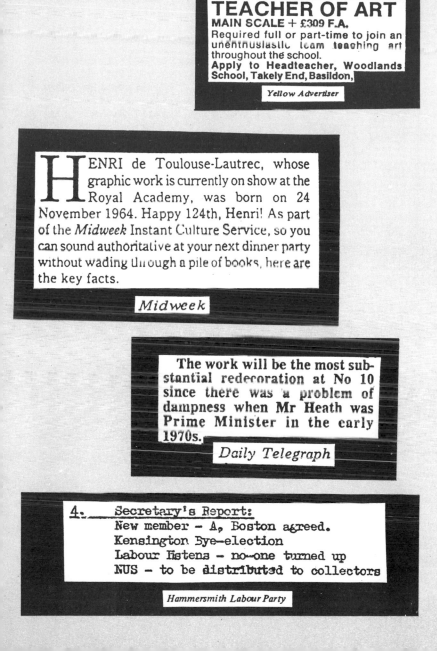

**TEACHER OF ART**
MAIN SCALE + £309 F.A.
Required full or part-time to join an
unenthusiastic team teaching art
throughout the school.
**Apply to Headteacher, Woodlands
School, Takely End, Basildon,**

*Yellow Advertiser*

HENRI de Toulouse-Lautrec, whose
graphic work is currently on show at the
Royal Academy, was born on 24
November 1964. Happy 124th, Henri! As part
of the *Midweek* Instant Culture Service, so you
can sound authoritative at your next dinner party
without wading through a pile of books, here are
the key facts.

*Midweek*

The work will be the most substantial redecoration at No 10
since there was a problem of
dampness when Mr Heath was
Prime Minister in the early
1970s.

*Daily Telegraph*

4.    Secretary's Report:
      New member – A. Boston agreed.
      Kensington Bye-election
      Labour listens – no-one turned up
      NUS – to be distributed to collectors

*Hammersmith Labour Party*

**LARRY ADLER**
*Restaurant Critic*

*Boardroom Magazine*

**8.30 NATURE**. First of two reports on lead-free petrol. It's well known that it damages children's brains and generally isn't good for you, but why is it not more freely available?

*The Independent*

# YORK SYMPATHY ORCHESTRA

**Leader Catherine Van De Weyer
Conductor John Godfrey
Soloist Robert Melling
Piano**

*York Evening Press*

There are far fewer misprints (though a growing number of spelling mistakes and grammatical errors: the fault of our education system rather than the industry). There have been a spectacular improvement in the quality of photo-reproduction, and this in turn has led to a more adventurous choice of photos.

*Paul Johnson, The Spectator*

ABOVE: Joint-Master and huntsman Mr Tony Carter, whipper-in Johnny Botham and joint-huntsman John Smith at the meet at Weald.

# Old Berks

ABOVE: (From left) Television racing commentator Richard Pitman, Joint-Masters Mr John Bosley and Mr Michael Green.

*Horse & Hound*

## Pope to Benin

**Rome:** The Pope arrives in Africa today, visiting Benin, where he will meet practitioners of voodoo, Uganda and Sudan.

---

She also revealed how she spent three evenings drinking with the England team at the Red Loin Inn in Rothley, not far from Nottingham, where the Test took place.

*The Telegraph Calcutta*

---

Further difficulties arose early yesterday morning, when a viola owned by Charles Maguire of the RTE Concert Orchestra was blown up in a controlled explosion carried out by the Army in Cork. The orchestra is performing at the Opera House with the INB.

*The Irish Times*

---

Sick pay, holiday pay and even maternity benefits coupled with the variety and flexibility of temporary work has meant that many women in Bromley now choose to 'tempt' on a permanent basis.

*Bromley and Hayes News Shopper*

The present crisis was sparked off two weeks ago when Mr Haughey moved towards a change in the law after the Irish Family Planning Association was fined for illegally selling condoms at the Virgin Megastore in Dublin.

*Daily Telegraph*

**VIEWING**

By appointment only, through Hill & Morrison (0256 702892).

**DIRECTIONS**

From Junction 6 of the M3 follow the signposts to Basingstoke, at the first roundabout turn left (Alton) and continue to the next roundabout, turn left again (Alton) and then go straight over the Venture roundabout (Alton) underneath the motorway and take the first right hand turning signposted to Cliddesden which you will then come into after about a mile. Continue past the village pond and Owl Cottage will be found after approximately 200 years on your left hand side.

Joe Jagger — son of the famous rock star, but now seeking publicity in his own right.

*Chatham News*

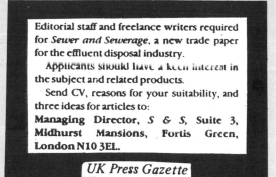

Editorial staff and freelance writers required for *Sewer and Sewerage*, a new trade paper for the effluent disposal industry.

Applicants should have a keen interest in the subject and related products.

Send CV, reasons for your suitability, and three ideas for articles to:

**Managing Director, *S & S*, Suite 3, Midhurst Mansions, Fortis Green, London N10 3EL.**

*UK Press Gazette*

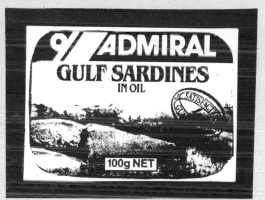

**RELATIONSHIP COUNSELING**

Dennis Thatcher, MFCCI

(415) 995-2916

Introductory Session $30

AIR CHINA INFRIGHT MAGAZINE
The 2nd Issue, Nov. 1989

Adviser: YANG SHUNZUN, YUZO NAKANISHI
Producer: HOU-YUXIANG, TAKESHI AOKI
Chief editor: YE DONGCHENG

## MA in MODERN EUROPEAN THOUGHT

Options in Fraud, Nietzsche, Aesthetics and Philosophy of Science.

---

But the fact that Mr Kinnock is still — in political terms — a young man, opens another avenue. He is in charge. He cannot be sacked. The worst thing that can happen to him is defeat in 1991 and the obscurity of an early bath.

*Grauniad*

---

## SINDEN'S OSCAR

Donald Sinden, whose acting career spans more than 45 years, makes his debut next month as a director in London's West End. He is to direct Dame Wendy Hitler as Lady Bracknell in a new production of Oscar Wilde's "The Importance of Being Earnest".

*Dublin Evening Press*

---

## OBITUARY

We record with regret the death of Ron Deadman, at the age of 68. He wrote several influential books on the teaching of reading and creative writing and was a features editor of *The Teacher* from 1961–1967 and editor of the former *Teacher's World* from 1967–1976.

*Education*

**JUNE 23**    **THE WINTERS TALE**
*&* **The Festival of Sheepshearing**
**in the gardens beside the river**
by W. Shakespeare
Sponsored by Rank Xerox plc

*Newbury Weekly News*

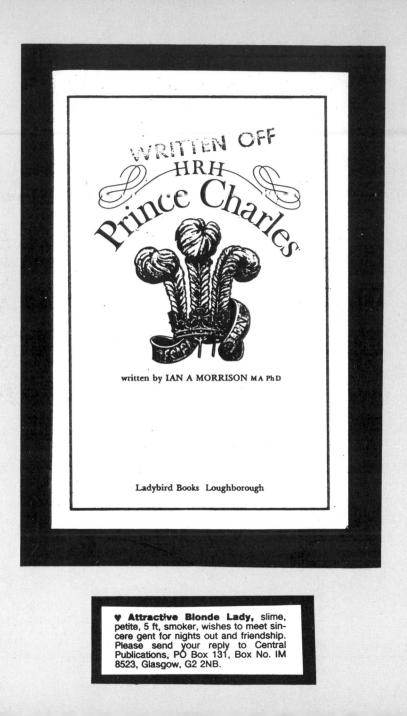

# WRITTEN OFF
## HRH
# Prince Charles

written by IAN A MORRISON MA PhD

Ladybird Books  Loughborough

## Cambridge Blue

This superb little Cambridge terrace pub has become the first tied house of Nethergate Brewery. The full range of Nethergate beers is always available - IPA, one of the best session ales around; the consistently fine Bitter and the wonderfully complex Old Growler. There are usually two guest beers (Guernsey Mild was spotted recently) and a real cider. Fortunately little else has changed. Gov'nor and Monster Raving Looney, Nick Winnington is still there, his enthusiasm for real ale means the pub has cocked up over 300 different beers in 2 years. Excellent food is available every session except Sunday evening. The pub has a Petanque pitch in the large back garden and is looking for challengers; ring Nick or Dave on Cambridge 61382 if you're interested.

*Ale Magazine*

Episode one of Coronation Street went out on a Friday night of December 9, 1960, with Violent Carson, Doris Speed, Pat Phoenix and William Roache in the cast.

*Glasgow Evening Times*

We will both praise and criticise without reference to a party line. Our campaigning will emerge from our rt-steve-usrting rather than the other way round.

*The Independent*

LYNN SYMINTON, of 45 Barleyknowe Lane, Gorebridge, was fined £80 for not having a television

**Breach and Assault**

*Peeblesshire News and St Ronan's Standard*

THE wedding of Miss Julia Dorothy Spencer and Mr Philip Turnock took place at Hailsham Parish Church.

The bride is the daughter of Mr and Mrs H. E. Spencer, of Battle Crescent, Hailsham. The bridegroom is the son of Captain and Mrs G. A. E. Turnock, of Victoria Road, Hailsham.

The bride wore a long dress of white organdie trimmed postman and a member of the Sussex Police Special Constabulary.

*Eastbourne Herald*

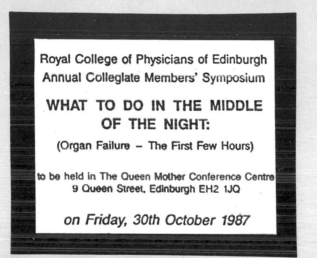

Royal College of Physicians of Edinburgh
Annual Collegiate Members' Symposium

## WHAT TO DO IN THE MIDDLE OF THE NIGHT:

(Organ Failure – The First Few Hours)

to be held in The Queen Mother Conference Centre
9 Queen Street, Edinburgh EH2 1JQ

*on Friday, 30th October 1987*

## Deaths

McLEOD. — On August 18, peacefully in hospital, Joseph Phillip McLeod, loving dad of Joe, father-in-law to Gwen, loving grandad to Jane, Ian and Kelly. Sadly pissed.   15E

*The Mail, Hartlepool*

### DRACULA

In the first of two horror films based on Bram Stoker's novel, Bela Lugosi stars as the vampire Count who leaves Transylvania and installs himself in a urined abbey in England.

*Wolverhampton Ad News*

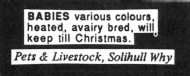

**9.35 PRISONERS OF CONSCIENCE.**
Ludovic Kennedy (*above*)
introduces a new group of prisoners

*Sunday Independent*

## Out of the pan . . .

A young man who impersonated a piece of bacon to amuse his friends was fined £20 after he admitted refusing to leave the area when told to do so by a police officer.

*Jersey Evening Post*

Mr Heseltine spent the weekend shooting ("he is the peasant's best friend. He doesn't hit anything," one aide .said on Sunday) near Oxford while the Tory party members of his Henley constituency. held an urgent meeting.

*Times of Zambia*

Snowtime in the foothills of the majestic Bavarian Alps . . . tempting prospects indeed of absolutely stunning winter scenery, with soaring peaks, dense pine forests and chalet-style cottages serenely draped in pure shite.

*Greenwich & Charlton News*

# A Valentine's Night Concert

*and your chance to view
hearts, flowers and genital jewellery*

at

## Royal Festival Hall

### Wednesday 14 February 7.30 pm
# ROYAL PHILHARMONIC
# ORCHESTRA

*Daily Telegraph/Times/Indy*

Fare deal for the elderly and disabled.
Westminster spends over £3 a year on concessionary fares
for the elderly and those with disabilities and, despite scare
stories by our political opponents, is totally committed to
maintaining the scheme.

*Conservative handout: Westminster City Council Elections*

# Shatner wins
William Shatner,
better known as Captain
James Kirk of Star Trek,
won an earthly court
battle yesterday in a
dispute over breeding
rights to a stallion. A
judge ruled that Shatner
had not agreed to a
lifetime breeding
agreement with
Lexington horsewoman
Linda Johnson.

*South Wales Echo*

Emperor Hirohito of Japan.

*The Indy*

## Surf's up

AD from the Falmouth Packet:
"Unspoilt country farmhouse in
lovely position. With expensive
coastal views."

*Daily Telegraph*

However, it is not just the physical deprivation of not
peeing from a window which has gone. Some feel that
they are being caged and, as such their freedom is
being restricted. Its a very sad situation for all concerned.

Police were jostled and kicked and one
constable was injured after being attacked
by a van inside a police man and later at
a police station.

*The Oxford Times*

# OVERSEAS TRAINING

OUR EMPLOYEE MR. IBRAHIM
ABDUL KARIM, OMANI
NATIONAL, HAS SUCCESS-
FULLY COMPLETED A
TRAINING COURSE ON LOSS
OF PROFIT, IN DOHA.

**OMAN UNITED INSURANCE CO. S.A.O.**

P.O. Box 4522 Ruwi, Sultanate of Oman - Tel.: 703990 - Telex : 3652 OUI ON

*Oman Daily Observer*

## Fisherman's tale

Earl Howe, Parliamentary Secretary for Agriculture, apologised to the Lords last night for making the wrong speech on the Sea Fish (Conservation) Bill, although no one seemed to have noticed.

*Daily Telegraph*

## Customs tax immoral earnings

The Customs are mounting a campaign to bring more prostitutes into the VAT net. Spokespersons would not reveal details of their methods of investigation, but it is expected that credit card analysis will play a role, since many brothels accept credit cards. It was made clear that Excise men would not personally sample the supplies of services (as they do in restaurants) and it is believed that they will assess the value and extent of services provided by the number of callers and the length of time they stay.

*Accountancy Age* — 27 April 1989.

# THE AGE

## WE WERE WRONG

In Michael Barnard's column on Tuesday, in the sentence that ended, ". . . it is plain that alienation of child from parent, the destroying of love and lust between innocents, must be an inescapable concern", the word "lust" should have been "trust".

The mistake was made in production.

Prime Minister, Defence and Technology: Rajiv Gandhi; **Agriculture, Rural Development:** Buta Singh; **Energy:** Vasant Sathe; **Eternal Affairs:**

*The Times*

# OVER YOU GO WITH P&O

*Caravan Club Magazine May '88*

There is something special about Vienna music. It's a combination of the sound of the grand canal and the padding of the gondoliers, the majesty of the palace of the dogs, the richness and sweetness of the pastries that come from the same country.—R Hartland Rowe (Calgary Herald)

*Free Press Journal (Bombay)*

## Attack on Dr Runcie

IN future no anonymous accusations should be levied at any clergyman, whatever his rank in our church.

When this can take place it leaves a nasty taste in my mouth.

If the writer or accuser cannot or will not quote his name he bears no credence whatsoever.

ANGLICAN

*Huddersfield Daily Examiner*

MATT BLACK
Available in matt only

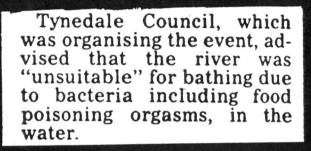

Tynedale Council, which was organising the event, advised that the river was "unsuitable" for bathing due to bacteria including food poisoning orgasms, in the water.

*Newcastle Journal*

## COURT AND SOCIAL

*The Daily Telegraph*

BUCKINGHAM PALACE
August 3rd
The Prince Edward this evening attended the Champagne Mumm Admiral's Cup Ball at Northwood House, Cowes. Her Royal Highness was received on arrival by Her Majesty's Lord-Lieutenant for the Isle of Wight (The Lord Mottistone).

Captain William McLean was in attendance.

GENTLEMAN FARMER 36 —
divorced, 6ft., dark haired, he
likes horses, sport, driving and
his home, seeks a happy, easy
going lay, aged 25-36 who e-
joys life.

*Brentwood, Billericay & Wickford Advertiser*

ExChief     Superintendent
Derek Owen, now co-ordinator
of the Birmingham Anti-Theft
Group, said: " In 37 years
police experience I've never
seen  anything

*Daily Express*

Mr Kinnock does not accept
all  the  criticisms,  reckoning
that he has around him the
nucleus of a potential Cabinet.
    But he accepts the need for
further improvement, and is
ready to take into account the
tactics agreed at the one-day
Shadow Cabinet session when
he reshuffles Labour's team in
late November.
elderly and geriatrics will be
on an unprecedented scale in
the decade ahead.

*Daily Telegraph*

# ACEADEMIC PRODUCTION EDITOR

The Academic Division of Unwin
Hyman is looking for an experienced and enthusiastic Production-
Editor to produce books on eco-
nomics, finance, business studies
and human geography. The job
involves the control of each stage
of the book's production from the

*Grauniad*

CHINESE Wang Jie undertakes a delicate muff dive in the team competition of the Pan Pacific synchronised swimming championships. The Chinese team finished fifth in the overall competition. (Reuter radiophoto)

*Arab Times*

**PYRFORD £169,500**
A large detached family property offering good accommodation including 4 beds, 2 baths, 3 receps and double garage. For all you keen golfers, this property backs onto West Byfleet Squash Club. Byfleet 48901.

*The Review*

Lord Rees-Mogg admitted that some of his preconceptions about the incidence of sex and violence on television had not been fulfilled since he began monitoring programmes last September.

"I have been learning on the job.

*Daily Telegraph*

**FOUR MUSKETEERS, THE** (PG)
The sequel/continuation of The Three Musketeers starring Oscar Wilde, Raquel Welch and Richard Chamberlain.

*Maxwell Cable TV Guide*

The thieves made off in a white transit van. One is 5'10" with a moustache aged between 30 and 40 with a blue suit and red tie wearing a green waxed jacket.

His accomplice is about 6" tall with collar length spikey hair in his early twenties and was wearing a red tracksuit.

*Aylesbury Plus*

ASTRA van, C reg, excellent condition, damaged off side front, some parts available, clean throughout, hence £825 (no VAT). Kensworth

*North Thames Auto Trader*

Now legal experts at Colchester council have been asked to decide if the 1966 planning permission to use the land as an air-base is still valid.

If it is, the club hopes to move to Wormingford in early August.

"We are not flying in the face of planners," said club chairman, Mr Paul Ricc.

*Essex County Standard*

The late Leonard Bernstein won the best female R&B vocal performance.

*Mainichi Daily News*

Willie Carson, riding his 180th winner of the season, spent the last two furlongs looking over one shoulder, then another, even between his legs, but there was nothing there to worry him.

*Sporting Life*

## TOURIST RATES

|  | Bank Buys | Bank Sells |
|---|---|---|
| Australia $ ......... | 0.00 | 0.00 |
| Austria Sch ........ | 00.00 | 00.00 |
| Belgium Fr ......... | 00.00 | 00.00 |
| Canada $ .........4. | 00.00 | 00.00 |
| Denmark Kr ....... | 00.00 | 00.00 |
| Finland Mkk ....... | 0.00 | 00.00 |

*The Times*

## CRUELTY FREE SPAGHETTI BOLOGNESE

Stir in 1 teaspoon of yeast extract with the mince. Chop onions and mushrooms. Fry onions in the margarine (much nicer than oil). Cook till soft. Add mushrooms and mice, cook for 2 mins. Add everything else and simmer for 10 mins.

*Stevenage Animal Rights*

"It's incredible," said Mr Lingam. "It looks just like a man's penis and it's not like anything I've ever seen before.

*Sunday Sport*

# Avitoff

36 Hyde Road, Paignton (0803) 524908

*Gentlemen's Barber Shop*

# Help to find dog

FRIGHTENED by a firework on Tuesday of last week a toy-size Yorkshire terrier escaped from the garden of its Rock Ferry home.

The dog hasn't returned and the lady owner, a pensioner, is seeking the help of Globe readers

She said the dog is wearing a collar with identification

*Wirral Globe*

---

With the New Year celebrations starting tonight Chief Insp Jones appealed for people to enjoy themselves but to stop and think before attacking a police officer.

*Western Mail*

---

**DOG** Basket, burns logs or coal; £30.- 051-920 7268.

---

### B.E.L.C.H.
Requires a
## DEVELOPMENT WORKER

*South London Press*

A GANG of youths overturned two cars and vandalised a police vehicle in a disturbance in Gibbet Street in Halifax town centre last night.

Three people were arrested for breaching the peace but were released without being charged. A police spokesman said the youths were lacking normal parental control because their parents were at prayer during Ramadan.

*Yorkshire Evening Post*

She was then chauffered in an official motorcade along the Mall leading to Buckingham Palace where she met with the Queen for just over 30 minutes. She left the palace in a private car for her home in Dulwich, southeast London, waving and smelling at cheering crowds as she went.

*The Rising Nepal*

On the grounds that this alteration would be a boon to the elderly and the infirm, who find themselves in difficulty with stiles when trying to get a leg over,

*Mid Wales Journal*

C'est paradoxalement un homme sorti droit du moule "thatchérien", John Major, qui dirigera désormais la Grande Bretagne. A 7 ans, Major devient le plus jeune premier ministre britannique du 20ème siècle.

*Temolin de Dakar, Senegal*

## Duchess flies out

THE Duchess of York, 8 months pregnant, flew to the US yesterday to see her stepfather Mr Hector Barrantes, 51, who is ill.

*Sunday Telegraph*

Security was stepped up, with hundreds of extra police and troops on duty, after news of her visit was leaked to two Irish Sunday newspapers. She decided to go ahead with the trip after security chiefs hastily assessed the risks.

She was flown to Belfast city centre by helicopter by IRA guerillas. *(Reuter)*

*Times of Malta*

TORQUAY: Bargain Breaks (any 4 days.
3 nights) £39.50. Full English breakfast, 5 course E. D. Friendly lice
Hotel.

*Wiltshire Times and News*

Motorists were stuck in a
five-mile traffic jam yesterday
after a glue tanker overturned
on the A355 at Slough, Berks.

*Daily
Telegraph*

A POTENTIAL Leicestershire cricket fan
came into the world this week.
 Samantha Jane Potter, who weighed in at
8st 4lb at Leicester General Hospital, is the
second child of Leicestershire County
cricket star Laurie Potter and his wife,
Helen.

*Leicester Mercury*

| MAMMALS | | |
|---|---|---|
| **ENDANGERED** | **THREATED** | **COMMOM** |
| Ocelote | Honey Aunteater | León breñero |
| Jaguar | Tapir | Anteater |
| Margay | Squirrel Monkey | Perezoso gris |
| Puma, Mountain Liom | | Tepezcuinle |
| Giant Aunteater | | Ring-Tailed Cat |
| Manatee | | |

*Illustrated Geography of Costa Rica*

**The last Thatcher produces piglets**

The RBST Bloodline Survey on the British Lop pig revealed only one Thatcher sow to be registered, the last in her line.

This great lady lives at the Sherwood Forest Farm Park and has rewarded the loving care and attention received there by producing a litter of eight piglets, 6 females and 2 males by her mate Aldens Duke 2nd.

*The Ark*

# ENCYCLOPÆDIA

## OF

# SEXUAL KNOWLEDGE

*By*

**Drs. A. COSTLER, A. WILLY**

**and others**

Oh dear. In our round-up last week of chartered accountant MPs we referred to Cecil Parkinson as 'a member cruncher'. It should have read 'number-cruncher'. Sub-editors, typesetters and printing gremlins alike are just wishing the ground would open up and swallow them.

*Accountancy Age*

To help it promote the rights of people with disabilities, the alliance wants to hear from women who have been pregnant since 1988

*NALGO News*

**MUSIC DEPARTMENT**

| | | |
|---|---|---|
| 1811 | Director of Music: Mr A Pither | 2780 |
| 1810 | Secretary: Mrs M Rose | 2781 |
| 10th | Teaching Room | 2786 |
| 4 | Teaching Room 1 | 2787 |
| 4 | Teaching Room 2 | 2787 |
| 1810 | Curator, Charles Moore Collection of Wind | |
| | Mr S Weston | 2056/2781 |

**11.0** **FILM: Percy.** Hywel Bennett is the recipient of a pioneering penis transplant in search of its donor in this limp 1971 comedy.
**12.55 Dick Spanner.**

*Grauniad*

● LAST week's letter 'Thatcher's selfish parkers' ended with the words, 'I'm Jack — bugger you!' This should have read, 'I'm all right, Jack —beggar you!'

*Oxford Courier*

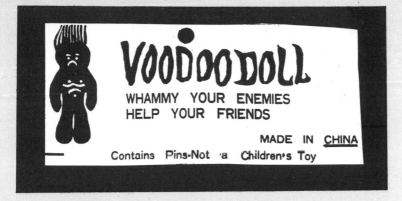

VOODOO DOLL

WHAMMY YOUR ENEMIES
HELP YOUR FRIENDS

MADE IN CHINA

Contains Pins-Not a Children's Toy

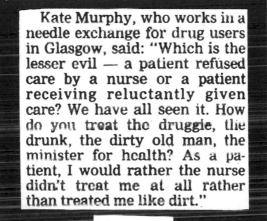

Kate Murphy, who works in a needle exchange for drug users in Glasgow, said: "Which is the lesser evil — a patient refused care by a nurse or a patient receiving reluctantly given care? We have all seen it. How do you treat the druggie, the drunk, the dirty old man, the minister for health? As a patient, I would rather the nurse didn't treat me at all rather than treated me like dirt."

*Grauniad*

R. v. Self    A        **JUDGMENT**
       Mr. Justice Garland: On July 10, 1991 in the Crown Court at

Court of Appeal
(Criminal Division)
   Kingston before His Honour Judge Wakley this appellant was tried on an indictment which contained three cunts.

*JUSTICE OF THE PEACE REPORTS*

**11.15 Lily Tomlin: The Film Behind The Show.** Ms Tomlin on the road with her shit show.

*Maidenhead Advertiser*

# Flashing warning

DOUCE Dunblane suffers the idignity this week of being described in a heading in the Stirling Observer newspaper as the "flashing capital" of Central region. Police have had to deal with 11 incidents of indecent exposure in the town over the past few months, compared with only four in Stirling.

The situation is put into some perspective by Central's chief constable, Ian Oliver, who is quoted by the newspaper as saying: "I am not too concerned. It tends to fall off in the winter."

*Glasgow Herald*

The offer of Ford cars to raise party funds is part of a plan by Larry Whitty, the party's general secretary, to drag Labour out of the red.

*Independent*

Nancy Reagan and Barbara Bush have written letters of encouragement to Kitty Dukakis, who has completed her first week in an alcohol treatment clinic. According to her father, Harry Ellis Dickson, the Massachusetts first lady is in good spirits.

*International Herald Tribune*

# MAJOR OUT TO KILL YELTSIN

AP                    Moscow

*New Zealand Herald*

**PLATT: He issued apology**

**MAJOR: Pleased at victory**

*Daily Express*

Keith Fletcher, the England team manager, defended his players by saying: "I do not see how you can go through India and not eat Chinese food.

*The Times*

Monday 18 and Tuesday, January 19 at 8.15 pm
HOUSE ON THE SEA PRODUCTIONS

~~CANCELLED~~

**DISAPPEARED**

**A new play by David Baldock**

*Harlow Playhouse*

Indeed, in this respect Dr Williams said he considered the service to be of more importance than the rival Swansea service in that Fishguard provided work for local people. The Fishguard service is 50/50 Welsh/Irish crewed, whilst the Swansea service employs Polish cucumbers.

*County Echo, Fishguard*

## BBC 1

**19.00 Nieuws**
**19.35 London Plus**
**20.00 Wogan**
Praatprogramma.

*Netherlands TV Guide*

The Princess of Wales, as patron of the National Hospital for Nervous Diseases, will attend a dinner for solicitors at Goldsmith's Hall, Foster Lane, at 7.55.

*The Times*

# Big increase in rouge directors

MORE than 250 rogue directors have been barred from Britain's board.

tors Disqualification Act, the Trade and Industry Secretary

demonstrate clearly our commit-

*Yorkshire Post*

FOUR policemen from Aycliffe and Sedgefield have received awards recognising 22 years of service with the force.

From left to right are DC Alan Courtney, Sgt Raymond Brown, Insp John Moore and Sgt James Walton.

All four were presented with their medals by Sir Anthony Milbank, High Sheriff of County Durham.

## Honours for police

*Aycliffe & Sedgefield Advertiser*

**9 00 News** (T), Regional News, Weather.

**9 30 Panorama** — The Bank That Didn't Add Up. Fred Emery report on the events leading to the biggest ever bank scandal — the collapse of BBCI.

*Daily Telegraph*

# Dead man fought when drunk

*The New Paper, Singapore*

"Some of the people who come here are really desperate. It cuts you up when you see some young unmarried mum who's money's run out, come in with her kid to pawn the wedding ring for £5 but that's how desperate some people can be.

*Grauniad*

# Australians
## lead in gas
### emissions

*The Independent*

9.30 **FILM** Poltergeist II (1986). The family have fled to Arizona and think they're safe until ...
11.00 **Neil Diamond's Christmas Concert**
11.45 **FILM** The Trea-

*Harrow Recorder*

This man's letters are extremely lucid but he is

**Roy Hattersley**

physically frail and walks with a frame. I cannot see how a 78-year-old man who walks with frame is such a danger to the public that he has to be locked up.

*Western Daily Press*

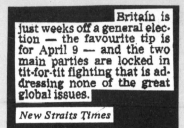

Britain is just weeks off a general election — the favourite tip is for April 9 — and the two main parties are locked in tit-for-tit fighting that is addressing none of the great global issues.

*New Straits Times*

# Cash offer for BBCI victims

*Today*

# Waste of time

Litter bins have been removed from lay-bys in Norfolk because "they increase the amount of rubbish", a council official said.

*Norwich Advertiser*

## Civic cheer

**GREAT-GRANDMOTHER Mrs Ethel Haynes, from Sutton Coldfield, is looking forward to a civic celebration to mark her 102nd birthday.**

**The Lord Mayor of Birmingham, Coun Bill Turner, will toast Mrs Haynes, who lives at Sutton Grange Nursing Home, Lichfield Road, at a barbecue there on Sunday,**

*Sutton Coldfield News*

```
J SAINSBURY PLC

       DORKING


                    £  .
  JS VANILLA I/CRM  1.29
  BUBONIC SQUEAK    0.79
  SCOTCH BROTH      0.31
```

*Time to celebrate — Michael Carr with his wife Georgina*

*Lancashire Evening Post*

**Capt P J A Balls and**
**Fräulein A Nützmann**
The engagement is announced between Capt Peter James Alexander Balls, Royal Green Jackets, eldest son of Mr Bryan Balls, of Atworth, Wiltshire, and Mrs Anne Balls, of Micheldever, Hampshire, and Andrea, daughter of Dr Heinz Nützmann, and Dr Marlis Nützmann, of Osterode, West Germany.

*Daily Telegraph*

## LOST

LOST on day of Glamaig Hill Race at Sligachan/Sconser — one half set false teeth. Further information from Sligachan Hotel.

*West Highland Free Press*

A ROSE period painting by Picasso, Acrobat and Young Harlequin, painted in 1905, was sold at Christie's in London last night for £20,900,000 million — a record for a 20th century work of art — to a bidder who was apparently Japanese.

*Grauniad*

BRIGHTON Council plan to avoid governmental rate-capping next year by cutting £3 off next year's spending. And that will be achieved through savings and increased income rather than any compulsory redundancies.

*Brighton & Hove Leader*

*Celebrating 40 years as a Band Leader*

# HUMPHREY LYTTLETON AND HIS BAND
● *A SPECIAL THREAT FOR ALL JAZZ FANS* ●

*Brighton Evening Argus*

**APOLOGY**

We would like to extend our apologies to Hallmark Cards for any offence caused by the feature *Creators of Crap*. None was intended and we would like to thank Hallmark for their help whilst researching the feature.

*Ms. London*

---

The murder of the charismatic Bishop on October 19, 1983, was cataclysmic for this small and intimate island society. Hard on its heels came the invasion by the US, which had long been grinning for the leftwing regime.

*Grauniad Weekly*

---

● Nine men have appeared in court after the Hackney poll tax riot.

One was sent to an attendance centre for 36 hours for growing tomatoes, another was fined £250 for spitting at a police officer and a third £50 for disorderly behavior.

*Nottingham Evening Post*

---

JOHN CHILES is the Conservative candidate for Tadworth and Walton Ward, where he has lived for 24 hours.

*Surrey Mirror*

**FLATTERING . . . Alec Stewart drives confidently before England's collapse**

*Sunday Express, Scotland*

But he refused to discuss his relationship with model Donna Rice, which forced him to pull out once.

*Oracle*

# Accused

A MAN went before Dorking magistrates yesterday charged with destroying property.

Martin Sheeran (18), a demolisher, of Horley, was remanded on unconditional bail until December 7.

*Dorking Advertiser*

Monday 13th June
Saturday 18th June 1988
Performances at 7.30pm

## *PAGE THREE GIRLS*

*The Sexplicit Adult Comedy*
Tickets: £6.50, £5.50, £4.50
Concessions Mon evening
2 for the price of 1
Parties 1 in 15 free
NOT SUITABLE FOR ADULTS

*Bristol Journal*

John Fox, writer, artist and founder of Welfare State International, has agreed to bed guest speaker at the January meeting. WFI have had an enormous impact on public theatre in this country, and John Fox's guiding spirit has been one of the prime reasons.

*Northern Playwrites' Newsletter*

"They have been suggesting that for some time. It's all rubbish. It's fiction." His comments followed claims that the Prince has been secretly Mrs Parker-Bowles for more than a decade, and as often as once a week.

● Camilla Parker-Bowles

*Evening Gazette*

If we are lucky we will see duck boys bringing their ducks home, men massaging their cocks on the road, cow boys taking grass. Yes it is a wonderful experience. Don't miss it during your visit to the island of gods, Bali.

*Tunas Indonesia*
*Tours & Travel*

"It is not sensible to encourage people to believe that we can go on sinsibly producing cola for which there is no market, for which there are no customers. People cannot have it all ways. They cannot press the prime minister and his colleagues for leadership and then say it should have been postponed or i should have been wrapped up differently."

*Douglas Hurd, reported in The Times*

**8.30 WORLD IN ACTION.** Documentary. *See Tonight's Choice.* 4875.

**9.0 HEAD OVER HEELS.** Camilla is far from happy when a princess arrives at the academy. **(T)** 9383.

*Daily Express*

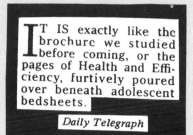

IT IS exactly like the brochure we studied before coming, or the pages of Health and Efficiency, furtively poured over beneath adolescent bedsheets.

*Daily Telegraph*

The condom company **Durex** made its first thrust into marketing its product in Ireland with a reception to launch a range of new improved condoms at the Conrad Hotel last Thursday afternoon. The managing director of Durex in The United Kingdom, **Gareth Clarke (ex Smurfit Group)**, said

"We don't want to push anything on Irish people

*Sunday Tribune*

# SMOKING KILLS
**Health Departments' Chief Medical Officers**

*Evening Standard*

THE parents of Yealmpton evangelist John Cornelius are celebrating this week after hearing he had been cleared of spreading Christian propaganda in Turkey.

His father Michael said: "It is great news. It's the answer to all our prayers."

*South Hams Gazette & Dartmouth Chronicle*

## Correction

WE have been asked to point out that in an article in Friday's Gazette on the proposed conversion of St. Gregory's Presbytery in South Shields, a sentence attributed to planners should have read: ". . . and that acute psychotics, alcoholics and drug users will NOT be taken in."

*Shields Gazette*

The programme winds up with Robert Parkin, a landscape designer from Hereford, marching through clouds of midgets to watch Scottish otters playing

*Manchester Evening News*

£102,950. KENTISH TOWN, NW5. An extremely elegant and light two bedroom raised ground floor flat in a very imposing period house. Conveniently situated for Northern Ireland underground buses and shops. Comprising reception, kitchen, bathroom, two double bedrooms, roof terrace, gas central heating.

*Advert, Ham & High*

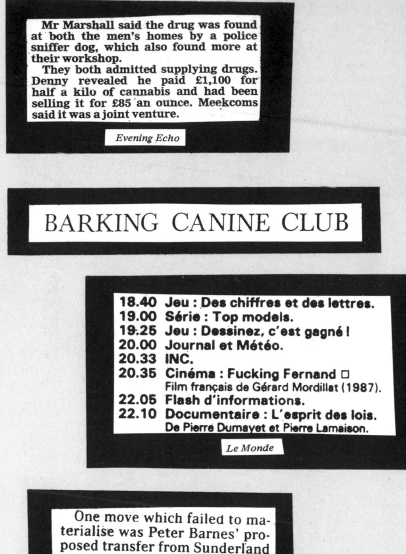

Mr Marshall said the drug was found at both the men's homes by a police sniffer dog, which also found more at their workshop.

They both admitted supplying drugs. Denny revealed he paid £1,100 for half a kilo of cannabis and had been selling it for £85 an ounce. Meekcoms said it was a joint venture.

*Evening Echo*

# BARKING CANINE CLUB

18.40 **Jeu : Des chiffres et des lettres.**
19.00 **Série : Top models.**
19.25 **Jeu : Dessinez, c'est gagné !**
20.00 **Journal et Météo.**
20.33 **INC.**
20.35 **Cinéma : Fucking Fernand** □
        Film français de Gérard Mordillat (1987).
22.05 **Flash d'informations.**
22.10 **Documentaire : L'esprit des lois.**
        De Pierre Dumayet et Pierre Lamaison.

*Le Monde*

One move which failed to materialise was Peter Barnes' proposed transfer from Sunderland to **Stockport**. Barnes was held up in a traffic jam and failed to sing in time.

*The Daily Telegraph*

Honeymoon couple... John Major ends his holiday visit to Maine after thanking President Bush 'for the leadership you have given to the free world' during a tumultuous period. An effusive Mr Bush told the Prime Minister: 'What a pleasure it has been to have you. Time has flown by. We have done an awful lot of business together.'

**SALES.REP.** for small business & Secretarial company to establish new accounts in Leigh area, age 25 plus, scar essential. Tel.0942-609628.

*Bolton Evening News*

Fergie communicates with patient Mr. Alistair Arthur, who has speech difficulties.

*Chatham, Rochester & Gillingham News*

**NEEDLESS ACUPUNCTURE.**
225 4825.

*Edinburgh Advertiser*

Mr Major has enough problems without adding that of a Cabinet Minister whose pubic image has been reduced to that of a foolish Lothario.

*Today*

# West Ham debate what they can do to change Dicks

*The Times*

# ALSO AVAILABLE FROM
# PRIVATE EYE • CORGI

### THE 2ND SECRET DIARY OF JOHN MAJOR

In the second instalment of his not inconsiderably Secret Diary, John Major again takes us behind the scenes of the great adventure known as Majorism.
£4.99

### A GNOME IN PROVENCE
### or
### TWO YEARS IN PRIVATE EYE

is a wonderfully rich crop from Lord Gnome's famous joke harvest. As ever it is a fine blend of cartoons, parodies and spoofs with its unmistakable sour grape and bad taste.
£4.99